Living Your Big Juicy Life

Living Your Big Juicy Life

The Secrets To Having More Love, Joy And Success

Michael Tarby

Dedication

To my Father: You have been a silent guiding light who has shown me that people can truly change. Thank you for showing me the beauty of peace, forgiveness and generosity. I love you and appreciate all the support you have given me through the years.

To my miniature dachshund Pebbles: Thank you for being my soulmate. You have shown me I am capable of unconditional love and it is absolutely wonderful. Daddy misses you and I cannot wait to see you again on the Rainbow Bridge.

Table of Contents

Preface

Welcome and congratulations! Congratulations? But you might say you haven't done anything yet. Yes you did, you bought this book, and that must mean you are looking for more from your life. That must mean you are ready to make some changes in your life so you can be happier. I think that deserves a quick pat on the back. You are awesome. Way to go!

So you might be wondering what a Big Juicy Life is anyway. How can your life be juicy? Well, the dictionary defines juicy as something that is lucrative, succulent, rich in interest, sensational, colorful, titillating, seductive, and satisfying. Doesn't that sound delicious? Soon you will be using those words to describe your life!

In simpler terms, living a Big Juicy Life means your life is filled with love, joy and success. When that happens, your life will be all that you ever dreamed of and nothing will be unattainable. You will see and experience the world around you like never before. You will feel energized and be unstoppable. Are you ready to start living the life of your dreams?

In this book, I am going to give you the secrets that will change your life forever. It does not matter where you are in your life right now; these principles will help you find more love, joy and success. They will work for everyone, and you can start using them today!

Let's take a look at some of the secrets you will learn in this book:

- You will learn how to love yourself and know that you are enough

- You will discover what the life of your dreams actually looks like

- You will stop procrastinating and learn to get things done

- You will be able to look within and find answers to all your questions

- You will know how to quickly and easily bring more happiness into your life

- You will not fear change anymore and you will take control of your life

- You will believe that you can do and be anything you desire

- You will learn to have better romantic relationships by looking within

- You will learn to get what you want by just asking for it

- You will learn that money is best spent on experiences

- You will learn to incorporate laughter into your daily life

But wait, there's more! You will learn a lot more secrets in this book. This book will also show you how to take advantage of the endless opportunities for you to have more love, joy and success.

That Sounds Great, How Do I Make It Happen

Acquiring knowledge is vital to making changes in your life, but it is just one aspect of personal growth. You must put this new knowledge into action. It is a necessary step that many other self-help, motivational type books do not teach. It's a good thing that this book is special. In this book, I will show you how to put these new concepts to use in your daily life. At the end of each chapter, I will offer you an action plan to help you get the most out of that chapter's lesson.

The more action plans you incorporate into your life, the more energized you will become. Once you see the success and positive effect of using the action plans, you will look forward to each new principle. Each new principle will allow you to build on the previous one. Soon you will be taking different actions and you will be getting different results than in the past. And that my friend is where all the magic happens.

Incorporating these action plans into your life is important for you to fully benefit from this book. Don't be like some people I know and just read the book and never do the exercises. I am just kidding of course. Do only what you feel comfortable with.

This Is Your Personal Journal

I encourage you to write in this book and use it as a guidepost for your personal growth. It is important for you to be as honest and open as you can when doing the exercises. Do not feel like you have to impress anybody or look for the right answers. As a matter of fact, there are no right or wrong answers. Just allow yourself the freedom to be able to express yourself fully and from your heart. The more you are able to do that, the more you will gain from this book.

Learn From My Experiences

We are going to have a great time together on your journey to living your Big Juicy Life. Along the way, I will make you laugh, make you smile, and make you see your life like never before. One of the ways I am going to do that is by sharing my personal stories with you. They are examples of some of my greatest successes and also some of my biggest challenges and failures. It is through the combination and contrast of my varied life experiences that I gained the knowledge I am going to share with you. They will help you understand the main points of each chapter and see how they relate to real life.

Many Aha Moments In This Book

Now let me forewarn you. While reading this book, you are going to experience a lot of "Aha moments". An "Aha moment" is when you suddenly come across something that makes you happy. I am not talking about discovering a twenty-dollar bill in your old jeans pocket, but more like a sudden awakening of something profound. It could be a realization that the answers to your biggest questions were right in front of you the entire time. It could be a new way of looking at things that you never considered before. It could be a new way of doing something that will give you more opportunities for love, joy and success. Good things are in store for you!

Feel Free To Jump Around

One of the great things about this book is that you do not need to read the chapters in order. Each one can stand on its own without having to read the previous or subsequent chapter. Feel free to be a rebel and jump around to the chapters that resonate with you the most. Just promise me you will read the entire book, I trust you.

You Can Have The Life Of Your Dreams

Congratulations on beginning this journey to have more love, joy and success in your life. You are an amazing being and you deserve it. Even though we have never met, I do know this; it is possible for you to live a happier and more fulfilled life. This book will show you how to change your thinking, change your actions, and change your life.

We are all in this experience together, and it is my privilege to offer you a helping hand. I look forward to your journey and I know that you will succeed. I hope to meet you sometime in the future and hear how this book has made a difference in your life. Now let's get juicy.

Introduction

I am happy and honored that you are going to let me help you have more love, joy and success in your life. Since we are going to be spending some time together and I am going to be sharing my deepest and darkest secrets with you, I think we should get to know each other a little better, I'll go first.

I was born and raised in central New Jersey, and no, I don't sound like Rocky Balboa. In 1998, I moved to Las Vegas and have been living here ever since. I have had a great life so far. It has been filled with excitement, romance and success. My life is an amazing example of someone living the life of their dreams, or so it seemed.

Let me tell you about some of the fun and exciting jobs I've had. I was a police officer for 14 years. I have felt the adrenaline rush of being in high speed car chases, being on the SWAT team and knocking down doors in drug raids. I was also an actor and a model. I appeared in several commercials and worked as a performer on the world famous Las Vegas strip. I was a flair bartender, and flipped bottles at one of the best bars in the world. I am currently a professional speaker and recently received a standing ovation from an international audience of over 240 people.

In many areas of my life, I have been an overachiever. I have been quite successful in school. I have a bachelor's degree in Criminal Justice and am also board certified in Radiography. I graduated with a 4.0 GPA and received several scholarships and awards. I was the class president in college and also in the fourth grade. They were only slightly different.

In my personal life, I was good looking, funny and charismatic. I had lots of girlfriends and didn't have any trouble getting dates. I was fun to be around and was usually the life of the party. I had many good times traveling all around the world with my friends. I lived my life in the fast lane and was always going somewhere or doing something.

Now if I just stopped right here, you might think I would be the perfect person to teach you how to live the life of your dreams. It would seem like I had the life that many would envy. The truth is there was another side to my life that nobody ever saw. My life was not as glamorous and shiny as it appeared. I struggled with low self-esteem, I was lousy in relationships, and I could never seem to find a sense of happiness that would last. My life seemed to be like two opposite sides of the same coin.

It is the contrast of living a full and happy life in some areas and struggling in others that has allowed me to gain the knowledge I am going to share with you. In this book, I will not only share some of my biggest successes with you, I will also share my struggles and mistakes. And believe me, I have made plenty of mistakes. If you ever feel like beating yourself up, you can take comfort in knowing I probably have made more blunders than you.

The good news is I am still alive and I am in the best spot in my life that I have ever been. I am the happiest, the most self-loving, and the most open I have ever been. It has taken me longer than I would have liked to finally get here and I wish I did not experience so much pain along the way, but the truth is it probably couldn't have happened any other way.

Everything in your life has led you to where you are currently in your life also, and wherever you are in your life right now, I want you to know you can be happier and more fulfilled. It is a beautiful thing that we can always choose where we want to go from here. I invite you to learn from my experiences, my mistakes and my life so that you may begin living the life of your dreams.

"Very little is needed to make a happy life; it is all within yourself, in your way of thinking."

- Marcus Aurelius

Chapter 1: You Can Have It All

Many of us feel it is not possible to live a life filled with as much love, joy and success as we would like. We think it must not be our destiny. We look at others' lives all around us and everyone else seems to be so happy. It seems like their lives are perfect. They come into work bragging about their new car, their new promotion, or how their partner made them heart shaped pancakes for breakfast. It can stir up a lot of conflicting emotions in us. We feel torn between wanting to congratulate them or wanting to spill a little coffee on their shoe when they are not looking.

The good news is we all can have the life of our dreams, and yes that definitely includes you! This isn't just wishful thinking or some type of Jedi mind trick, it is reality. It is time to stop thinking that others have everything they want because they possess qualities that you do not have. Nothing could be further from the truth.

You have all you need to have a great relationship, feel successful and be happy. You might be asking yourself if that is true, then why hasn't it happened yet, it's not like you haven't been trying. What are you missing? Let's start by clarifying a few things.

The roads to finding love, joy and success are winding. The paths to being happy and fulfilled do not follow a straight line. There are many twists, detours and a couple dead ends along the way. It seems like no matter how well you plan your life, there are unexpected situations that occur. Our lives are purposefully designed so that there are many surprises along the way. Life is like a box of chocol- never mind, you get the idea. But all of that is great because that is one of the reasons why life is so much fun.

It is through the magic of the unknown that makes life so interesting. The ever-changing ways your life unfolds guarantees that you will see new places, meet new people and have new experiences. It is through all those new interactions that give you unlimited opportunities for love, joy and success. The problem is you probably haven't been seeing the opportunities that have been right in front of you. It is time to open your eyes and see things in a new way.

You Are Not Stuck

Many times in life, we can feel like we are stuck. We feel like life is beyond our control and the odds are not forever in our favor. This feeling of being stuck can bring on a sense of frustration, lethargy and sadness. I am here to tell you a little secret; whisper this as you read it, it makes the secret seem even more profound. "You are not stuck, you have never been stuck and you never will be stuck."

The feeling of being stuck is just an illusion. It is purely a mind control trick. It is a game that your mind has been playing with you. Many times we feel stuck because of something that has happened in our past. We incorrectly believe that the past equals the future. Let me give you an example of how your mind can trick you into believing that you are stuck.

The Elephant And The Rope

Have you ever seen pictures or video of elephants standing outside of the tents at the circus? They usually have a rope tied around one of their legs and the other end is attached to a stake in the ground. The ropes are quite thin and flimsy. I always wondered why the elephant just doesn't break the rope and walk over to the concession stand. I think he would enjoy a bag of roasted peanuts in between shows.

It would be an easy task for the elephant to use its massive strength to either break the rope or pull the stake out of the ground. I wondered why the elephant doesn't realize it has all the power in the world to set itself free. What has happened to these amazing animals that they have forgotten how much power they have and allow themselves to be stuck?

Here is where it gets tricky. The way they train the elephant to stay in one place is by teaching it from a young age to give up. The way they do this is when the elephant is young, they put a chain around the elephant's leg and attach it to a stake in the ground. Even though the elephant tugs and pulls on the chain as hard as it can, it is not strong enough to break free.

After a while, the elephant stops trying to break free. It accepts its fate of being stuck anytime the chain is placed around its leg. Eventually the trainers do not even need to use a chain anymore, they can use a flimsy rope and that will have the same effect. What a dirty trick that is, huh. No wonder elephants get pissed off and storm through the town when they figure out they can break free from the flimsy rope and could have broken free much sooner.

Now here is the important part of the story. Even as the elephant grows from being a child into an adult, it never stops believing that whenever something is attached to one of its legs, it is powerless to overcome it and has to stay where it is. The elephant has been conditioned to keep reliving past experiences and does not realize things are different now. It does not realize it is much stronger than when it was a child. It does not know it has more power now and if it just tried one more time to break free, it would be successful.

The same thing can happen to you when you are bound by negative or limiting beliefs. Just because you had a negative or limiting experience in the past, it does not mean it will happen again. Tony Robbins has a great quote which sums this up, "The past does not equal the future."

The Past Does Not Equal Your Future

It is important for you to realize that your past does not equal your future. Just like the elephant, many of us can get bogged down in the beliefs that we are powerless to change our lives and affect our circumstances. The truth is you have the power to change anything and everything in your life. All you really have to do to change your life is decide to change it. Once you decide to change it, you can alter the way you think, the way you act and what you believe at any time you wish.

It does not matter what has happened in the past. It does not matter what happened five years ago, five months ago or even five minutes ago. What happened in the past does not guarantee the same thing will happen again. Realize it is always up to you when you will decide to give up or when you will tap into your personal power.

It is time for you to break free from your negative and limiting beliefs that no longer serve you. You need to know that you are free to explore the world and discover all the infinite possibilities for you to live a happy and fulfilled life.

Change Your Thinking And Change Your Life

It is time for you to start embracing new beliefs, new philosophies and new strategies. It is by incorporating this new knowledge into your daily life that everything can magically change. It is important to start doing things differently if you want more love, joy and success.

It is quite ironic that even though many of us realize our actions are not bringing us what we desire, we continue doing the same thing. That sounds like the definition of insanity, doing the same thing over and over again and expecting a different outcome. It is time for you to stop the insanity and consider there are better ways of understanding yourself, seeing life and taking action.

It might feel awkward at first to begin accepting new knowledge as the truth. It can be scary to let go of beliefs that you have carried for quite some time. Let me give you an example. Can you imagine how unsettling it must have been when people realized the world was not flat? I bet some people embraced this new knowledge and went out and bought a boat. Sailing sounds like a lot more fun when you don't have to worry about falling off the edge of the world. On the other hand, I am sure there were people who still insisted the world was flat and refused to believe this new knowledge. I bet you those were also the same people who believed the moon was made of cheese.

It is by embracing new knowledge that having more love, joy and success is made possible. The key is to have an open mind and accept the possibility that there are better ways of achieving your goals and desires. When your thinking and beliefs are more free flowing and you become flexible in what you hold as true, it will open up many new opportunities for you to live a happier and more fulfilled life.

Chapter Summary

- You can have the life of your dreams
- It is by meeting new people, seeing new places and having new experiences that you will find more love, joy and success
- Change your thinking to change your life
- Take different action to get different results
- Your past does not equal your future
- You are never stuck

Action Plan

List some ways that you feel stuck in your life.

Example: I feel stuck in a dead-end job.

1. _____

2. _____

3. _____

4. _____

The good news is that you are not stuck; you can change anything and everything in your life. You just need to change your beliefs and see how truly powerful you are.

List some things you used to believe were true, but now believe something different.

Example: I used to believe that I had to have a college degree in order to get a good paying job.

1. _____

2. _____

3. _____

4. _____

Do you see that your beliefs can change over time? It is by embracing new beliefs that will allow you to have more love, joy and success.

Daily Action:

1. When you are feeling stuck, take a deep breath and realize that you have the power to change anything and everything in your life.

2. Be more open to suggestions for improving your life.

3. Look all around you for new clues on how to live a happier and more fulfilled life.

4. When you find yourself thinking about past mistakes and failures, change your focus to the present and think of what you can do today to be happier. Do not get hung up on your past. Remember, your past does not equal your future.

"You alone are enough. You have nothing to prove to anybody."

-Maya Angelou

Chapter 2: You Are Enough

There are many different factors that will determine the level of happiness you will experience in your life. Even though many people focus on money, love and material possessions, the most important factor is none of those. The biggest factor that will affect how happy you will be in your life is the way you feel about yourself. It is the way you feel about yourself that will either allow you to live the life of your dreams or make you feel like there is always something missing.

If you feel you are not good enough, not smart enough, or not attractive enough, those feelings set you up for a lifetime of doubt, struggle, and pain. When you have low self-worth, you will see the world and everything in it as being against you. You will easily find examples of when you are disrespected, mistreated and unloved. Those situations seem to reinforce the belief that you must not deserve love, joy and success. This perpetuates the vicious cycle of feeling unworthy.

Conquering this negative belief of not being enough is the single best thing that you can do to live the life of your dreams. Once you feel that you are enough, your whole world changes. You will be bold in taking chances, making things happen, and taking advantage of the endless opportunities to have all your dreams come true. Everything will seem to magically fall into place for you.

In this chapter, I will show you that the feeling that you are enough has to come from inside you. Nobody else can make you feel that way. People can help you see how great you are and encourage you to change your belief, but the only person who can make it happen is you. And before we go any further, I want you to know, YOU ARE ENOUGH!

The Symptoms Of Low Self Worth

There is no greater pain than the feeling of not being enough. This negative self-belief permeates your entire being and alters your perception of everything. It makes you unable to see all the goodness and glory that is within you. Instead, you only focus on what you are lacking.

Having low self-esteem makes it very easy to dwell on the wrongs that have been committed against you. You will continually relive painful memories of being disappointed, being disrespected, and being hurt. If these events happened in your childhood, it can instill in you a never-ending feeling of not being good enough.

When you feel you are not good enough, you will be inclined to be a people pleaser, sacrificing your own wants and desires for the sake of someone else's wishes. You will not feel secure in your own desires and will be easily swayed from your true dreams.

Having low self-worth also breeds low self-confidence. You will be hesitant in making decisions, big and small. You are inclined to be paralyzed with fear and are afraid of taking chances. Even though you are probably more successful than most in all areas of life, the fear of making a mistake can be gut wrenching. It does not matter how many successes you have had in the past, your self-worth hinges on each new decision you make.

When you have low self-esteem, you can be overly sensitive to perceived slights from all those around you. You tend to overreact and can feel like people are always purposefully and deliberately trying to hurt you. It can seem like every day is a struggle trying to not let people upset you.

You also carry an underlying feeling of anger. It will come from a sense of frustration that people do not appreciate all you are doing for them. It can seem like you are doing everything to be a good person, to treat others with respect and to make sure you do not hurt anyone. When those actions are not reciprocated toward you, you will feel cheated and upset.

If any of that rings true to you, take comfort in knowing that you are not alone. Feeling unworthy is a terrible emotion that many people experience, including me. I have struggled to overcome that feeling for most of my life. I finally had a breakthrough several years ago that allowed me to understand how to break the wicked spell of not being enough. Allow me to share my story with you.

Please Tell Me I Am Enough

I have had an amazing life so far. By most of society's standards, I have been a mover and a shaker. I made things happen and was successful in all areas of my life. I had great jobs, I had beautiful girlfriends, and I had any material thing I could desire. It looked like I was living a life that many would envy. The truth is there was a little secret that I always carried around that nobody else knew. That secret was I was not enough.

It didn't matter what I did or what I accomplished; I always felt like I was not good enough. There were brief moments of feeling worthy that popped up from time to time. Maybe it was finishing my bachelor's degree or winning an award here and there, but inevitably, I would be engulfed by the nagging feeling of still being unworthy.

I desperately tried to find the secret of how to feel like I was enough. I went to counseling, I read self-help books, and I even went to a psychic. It might sound silly, but I wondered if I was cursed at one point. It didn't make sense that I was having so much difficulty in feeling good about myself. I thought maybe I had angered a local gypsy and got the evil eye.

After I realized I was not cursed, I continued looking for the answers to free myself from my low self-esteem. I painstakingly analyzed every part of my life looking for when this terrible feeling began. I figured if I could trace it back to the beginning, I could then change it at its root.

I started to identify situations from my childhood that I felt contributed to my belief of not being enough. I remembered times when I was put down, shamed or felt unloved. I sat with those memories and tried to let them go. I was having difficulty with that because I struggled to make sense of why they happened in the first place.

During one of the lowest points in my life, I reached out to my father to ask him questions about the painful memories I had from my childhood. I was hoping he could help me see them in a different way, a less damaging way. Many times you hear adults say to children, "When you are older you will understand". I was looking to put that theory to the test.

My father agreed to sit down with me and answer any questions I had. Even though I was glad that he said yes to my request, I felt a little embarrassed. Here I was, a grown man in my 30's, having to tell my father I was still hurt from when I was a child.

When my father came over, I had a list of questions waiting for him. I asked him why he was harder on me than my sister and why it seemed like she was his favorite. I asked him why he was so quick to criticize instead of praise. I asked him why he was so cold and aloof at times. I also brought up memories I had of when he made fun of me or put me down.

My father listened to each question and did his best to remember the situations I described. He was honest and forthright in his explanations. He told me about his philosophies and thinking at the time. He explained that he believed that men were supposed to be macho back then. Men were not supposed to show much affection. He also believed that men were the strong leaders of the family, and that is one of the reasons he was harder on me than my sister. He also told me how his upbringing had played a part in his inability to show love and affection. After he had answered all my questions, he reflected on what I brought up and said he would do things differently if he had the chance to do them again.

As much as I appreciated his answers and could understand his explanations, I did not feel better. In fact, I was feeling much worse. His answers did not give me the relief I was hoping for. Even though I could now understand where he was coming from all those years ago, it still did not lessen my pain of feeling like I wasn't enough.

Suddenly I had an epiphany. I realized that he never told me I was enough in my life before. I thought that if my father finally told me I was enough; this weight I had been carrying around would finally be lifted. I had heard stories of people having breakthroughs with pivotal moments and conversations with their parents, and I knew that this was going to be one of those times.

I was bold in asking my father questions thus far, but the thought of asking him to tell me I was enough made me feel very unsettled. It was like the final reveal of the secret I had been carrying around for so long. I was also afraid my father would think I was a weak man. As uncomfortable as I was, I had to press forward and find the courage to ask to hear those words.

I began by telling him how I had done so many amazing things and had such high achievements in all areas of my life. I explained that even though I had done all those things, I still felt like it was not enough. I told him that I thought it would be helpful if he were to tell me that everything I had done in my life was enough, that I was enough.

My father immediately began listing some of the wonderful things he knew I had done in my life. As he was recounting my successes and accomplishments, my heart was racing and I could feel the uneasy anticipation of him going to say that I was enough. After a few more sentences, the words came out of his mouth. "You have done enough son, you are enough." I finally heard the words I had been longing to hear all my life. My father, the most influential man in my life, had just told me I was enough.

After hearing those words, it was like a ray of sunshine immediately broke through the clouds. I felt like a huge weight had been lifted off me and I could finally breathe. I could swear that the colors in the room seemed brighter. We both burst into tears and gave each other the best hug ever.

That is what I expected to happen, but the truth is none of it happened.

I sat there for a few seconds in complete disbelief. I was shocked that there was no big revelation. I did a quick mental check to make sure that I did in fact hear my father tell me I was enough. I was positive he said it. I wondered why I wasn't feeling the way that I thought I would. It was quite a letdown. It was like lighting a fire cracker and eagerly waiting for the bang, but it turns out to be a dud and you get nothing.

I thought maybe if I heard it a couple more times it would sink in and affect me. I asked him again to tell me I was enough. He smiled and repeated it, "Yes son, you are enough." I closed my eyes and waited for the miracle to happen, but the miracle never came.

I thought of asking him to say it a few more times, perhaps he could say it with a little more sincerity. Maybe if he said it with more emotion it would make the difference. But in my heart and soul, I realized that it wasn't going to matter what my father said, it wasn't going to change the way I felt about myself. From that pivotal moment, I realized an essential truth; it is only YOU that can free yourself from feeling like you are not enough.

I will always be grateful to my father that he was so supportive of me during that low period in my life. I should also add that my father is not the man he once was. Over the years, he transformed into a much more loving, affectionate and supportive person. After seeing what a different man my father became, he has been an inspiration that I could change for the better also. Do not believe that people can't change, they can and so can you.

Only You Can Free Yourself

I learned a lot from that experience with my father. It made me realize that the only person who can make you feel like you are enough is you. Often we spend so much time and energy on seeking external validation. We are constantly seeking approval and recognition from everyone around us. And even when we get the validation we are looking for, it is still not enough. We then believe we must need to do more in order to feel better about ourselves. This belief turns into a pattern of always striving for more, but never feeling any better. It is like trying to fill a bag with sand that has a hole in it.

The good news is that you don't have to continue experiencing the pain of low self-esteem. It does not matter where those feelings of low self-worth came from. It does not matter whether they came from your family, your friends, your peers, or anywhere else. The solution to feeling good about yourself is to change the way you see yourself. You need to change your beliefs and start seeing how awesome you really are.

You Can Change Your Beliefs

Your beliefs about yourself are the foundation of your life experience. Everything stems from what your beliefs are. Your beliefs will determine your perception, your emotions, and your reality. Some people think they can't change their beliefs. Nothing could be further from the truth. Whether you realize it or not, you are changing your beliefs all the time.

Think about some beliefs you had in the past that have changed over the years. Do you remember when you believed that the Easter Bunny was real, monsters lived under your bed, and the opposite sex had cooties? They all weren't true, right? On a side note, I did think girls had cooties when I was younger, but it was only because my classmate Susie Johnson had a bad case of head lice in second grade.

Once you embrace the fact that you can change your beliefs, you can start to identify the ones that are no longer serving you. You can then consciously and deliberately choose better beliefs. Remember, you get to choose what your beliefs are about anything and everything.

How To Believe Your Belief

When you have a belief, you will naturally look for reasons why that belief is true. If you think you are a failure, you will search for experiences from your past when you were not successful. Once you find those experiences, it is easy to embrace the belief that you are a failure. It might seem hard to see your worthiness any other way. It seems like the proof is right in front of you. It is like a twisted math equation that makes your belief an absolute truth; like this example; I have failed in the past = I am a failure.

The reality is many times you make assumptions that do not tell the whole story of who you are. Even though you have not been successful in every moment of your life, that does not mean you are a failure. For most people, it seems much easier to concentrate on all the negative things about ourselves rather than the positive. We are quick to point out our flaws instead of celebrating our gifts. We seem to focus on our mistakes rather than our achievements. It is no wonder we can feel so bad about ourselves, we are looking at the wrong things.

Once you start taking an honest look at your life, you will see that you have done more good than bad, you have had more successes than failures and you have brought more joy into people's lives than pain.

Just as you can focus on the negative experiences to bolster your belief that you are NOT enough, you can also use your positive experiences to begin believing that you ARE enough. There is evidence all around you that you are enough. Not only that you are enough, but you are more than enough! Once you begin to look for proof in your life that you are awesome, you will quickly find it.

How To Change Your Beliefs

The best way to change your beliefs is to challenge the ones that no longer serve you. The way you do this is to contradict the negative belief by substituting it with the opposite, or a more positive one. Let me give you an example. If you believe that you are a failure, try believing that you are a success. You can then look back in your past and find examples of when you were successful. You will quickly find proof that the belief that you are a success is not a lie, it is true.

Once you start seeing the proof of positive beliefs, you can begin letting go of all those negative beliefs you have been carrying around for so long. It is actually quite fun when you see how easy it is to replace all those negative beliefs with more positive ones.

Now that you have more beliefs to choose from, you can make a conscious effort to start reinforcing the positive beliefs instead of the negative ones. Whenever you find yourself embracing a negative belief, stop your train of thought and choose a positive belief. When you do that, it will immediately change your emotional state and make you feel more optimistic and positive.

Overcoming The Doubt

If you find yourself having difficulty with instilling your new beliefs of high self-worth and feeling good about yourself – it's ok – be gentle with yourself. Don't rush to make judgments that the new beliefs must not be true. Don't think that you are just fooling yourself by thinking you are worthy.

When you feel frustrated and seemingly torn between two conflicting belief systems, do not give up. Just keep challenging your negative beliefs. Ultimately you will see that they are not true and discover the proof of all the reasons why you are enough.

Over time, your bouts of doubt will decrease and you will be slowly tipping the scales into a more positive belief system. Soon, your positive self judgement will be the only one that feels true. Your feelings of low self-worth will now feel as foreign and false as when you first started to believe that you were wonderful. Don't give up, you will get there. And when you do, you will never have to go back to carrying the pain of low self-esteem. You can do it!

It's Time To Embrace Your Wonderful Self

When you start believing you are worthy, lovable and fantastic, it will seem like all of the sudden, the world has changed all around you. You will start noticing people treating you better than ever before. You will notice people smiling at you and starting conversations with you when they never spoke to you in the past. You will find yourself having more opportunities for love, joy and success without even looking for them. You might wonder what has happened.

There are subtle changes that often go unnoticed by us when we start feeling we are worthy. Your posture might change and you begin walking taller and with more confidence. You make eye contact with people when you talk to them and aren't afraid to smile at strangers. When you speak your ideas or opinion, your tone is more relaxed and assured. You are more comfortable in social situations and no longer fear rejection or judgment.

When you feel that you are enough, there is nothing you cannot do or achieve. It is time to embrace your wonderful self. It's time to start seeing yourself as the kick-ass dream maker that you truly are. All your dreams can now be reality. Everything can happen for you because YOU ARE ENOUGH!

Chapter Summary

- The way you feel about yourself is the biggest factor of how happy you will be in your life

- Conquering your negative self-beliefs is the single best thing you can do to have more love, joy and success in your life

- Only you can free yourself from negative self-beliefs

- You can change your beliefs

- You are a lovable, wonderful, and worthy being

- You are enough!

Action Plan

Write down some negative self-beliefs that you have been holding onto. Below your negative beliefs, write down the reasons why those beliefs are true.

Example: I am unlovable. It is true because my last romantic partner cheated on me.

Negative Belief: _____

Reasons why it is true: _____

_____

Negative Belief: _____

Reasons why it is true: _____

_____

Negative Belief: _____

Reasons why it is true: _____

_____

Negative Belief: _____

Reasons why it is true: _____

_____

Now write down the opposite of the negative self-beliefs you selected in the previous section. Below your positive self-beliefs, write down the reasons why those beliefs are true.

Example: I am lovable. It is true because I have lots of friends and family members that adore me.

Positive Belief: _____

Reasons why it is true: _____

_____

Positive Belief: _____

Reasons why it is true: _____

_____

Positive Belief: _____

Reasons why it is true: _____

_____

Positive Belief: _____

Reasons why it is true: _____

_____

Did you find reasons why both sets of beliefs are true?

Which beliefs made you feel happier, the positive or the negative ones?

Which beliefs did you resonate with as being the most true?

If you said the negative ones, you have been focusing on the wrong beliefs for too long. The good news is you can change that.

Daily Action:

1. Stop all negative talk about yourself, either with others or silently. It does no good to reinforce the negative beliefs you have been holding onto. Begin catching yourself saying negative things about yourself and say something positive instead. It might feel awkward at first, but it will get easier.

2. Be gentle with yourself. Do not beat yourself up if you occasionally slip into a negative belief pattern. Just keep catching yourself when you do it and challenge the negative belief until it no longer feels believable. Eventually your new positive self-beliefs will be the only ones that feel true.

3. In life, you will always find more of whatever you focus on. When you focus on positive self-beliefs, you will notice more situations in which you are being respected, admired and loved. You will be surprised at how easy it will be to find confirmations of what a wonderful and amazing person you are.

4. Keep a journal of events and situations that make you feel good about yourself. It could be when someone gives you praise, shows you love or appreciates you. Your journal will help you embrace the validity of your positive self-beliefs.

"The privilege of a lifetime is to become who you truly are."

- C.G. Jung

Chapter 3: What Are Your Wishes

Too many people go through life feeling unfulfilled and unsatisfied. Often they find themselves in places they did not anticipate being in, whether it is a dead-end job, a bad relationship, or getting shot out of a cannon at the circus. How is it that so many of us seem to find ourselves in places where we are not happy?

You would think it would be easy for us to identify what we want out of life and just go out and get it. The world is filled with endless opportunities to make all your desires become reality. The world truly is your personal playground, but we have been mired down in self-doubt and have let outside influences talk us out of going after our dreams.

We might become torn between what we truly want and what we think we should want. This sets us up for living someone else's life instead of our own. You might have difficulty even allowing yourself the freedom to question what you want out of your life without feeling guilty. You might feel that you must put others' needs and desires before yours. That is not the way to live the life of your dreams. You need to realize that you must come first.

It is only by putting yourself first that you will be able to live your life to the fullest. Some people might see that as being selfish. The truth is it is not. Once you bring more love, joy and success into your own life, you will naturally contribute more to the lives of others. It is the ultimate win-win formula.

In this chapter, you are going to learn how to become clear with what you really want out of life. I will show you how to use your heart as your compass when making decisions about which paths to choose. You will learn to forget the outside influences that can sway you from chasing your dreams. I will also show you how to use the amazing power of visualizing to help you find new opportunities for more love, joy and success.

Describe The Life Of Your Dreams

The first step to living your Big Juicy Life is to know what the life of your dreams actually looks like. In order to discover this, you need to begin by asking yourself some very important questions:

Who do you want to be?

What do you want to do for a living?

Where would you like to live?

What activities do you want to do in your life?

What kind of romantic relationship would be ideal for you?

When was the last time you asked yourself any of these questions? It is amazing how much time we spend going through life not knowing what we want. If you are not clear about your desires, how will you know what direction to go to find them? It would be like trying to find a treasure on a treasure map, but it is not marked with an "X". Where would you even begin to look?

When we are not clear about what we want, we can find ourselves drifting through life. It is no wonder that many people experience unhappy lives filled with jobs they hate, failed relationships, and a recurring sense of being unsatisfied. Without a clear direction, you are just haphazardly trying to find your happiness. It doesn't work very well. The good news is you have a tool which will help you determine what will bring you the most joy.

Let Your Heart Guide You

It is vitally important to become clear about what you want. This may sound, or seem easy to do, but it can quickly become confusing. When you begin to look at all the options you have in your life, there is often a battle that begins raging between your heart and your mind. Sometimes your heart is longing for something, but your mind jumps in and gives you all the reasons your desire is not practical, probable or obtainable.

In your past, which side usually wins out, your heart or your mind?

Many times, we rationalize away our true desires in order to be more practical. You might try to talk yourself into accepting something less than what you truly want. You try to convince yourself that this "less than" choice is just as good as your true desire. But in your heart, you know the truth. You really are settling for something less.

You are not here on this planet to settle for less. You are here to have exactly what you desire. There is no need to make excuses for what you want or listen to your mind giving you reasons why you do not need or deserve it. The mind can be one big party pooper sometimes. It is time to give your dreams a fighting chance. It is time to start listening to your heart instead of your mind.

Your heart is the most knowledgeable source for what will make you happy. Your heart is where your joy, love and excitement reside. We have allowed it to become silenced for too long. We have let the mind overrule the heart too many times in the past. It almost seems like your mind has Veto power over your heart. Your heart says "I want this" and the mind says "No, end of discussion." It's time to make your heart your primary decision maker.

When you tap into the feelings of your heart, you will find an unfailing compass that will guide you to living the life of your dreams. You can use your heart to find the best ways to be happy and also alert you to a change that is needed. Your heart will reveal your true feelings about everything that is going on in your life.

When you experience feelings of excitement, joy and hopefulness, you know you are on the right track. When you experience feelings of sadness, hopelessness and being defeated, you know you are on the wrong track. These feelings can help you determine if you are headed in the right direction or if you need to change course.

You can think of it as the childhood game of "Hot and Cold." Let me give you an example. If you start considering a job that doesn't suit you, your heart starts saying cold, you are getting colder. When you change course and begin looking at other job opportunities, your heart will say you are getting warmer. Then, when you find something you are really excited about, your heart will say you are red hot. You will know that you are in the right spot and have found the best option. Who knew that a childhood game held all the answers to life?

You will be surprised at how easy decision making will become when you start using your heart as your happiness compass. It might be difficult at first to resist the urge of being practical over your desire to be happy. Be patient with yourself and soon you will feel comfortable listening to your heart instead of your mind. Let me tell you a story about when I almost chose to be practical over being happy.

The Mobile Home Salesman

The year was 1998 and my life had fallen apart. I was looking for a change and was ready to go in a new direction in my life. I had family living in Las Vegas and decided to move there. Las Vegas was known as a town with 24-hour gambling, unlimited free drinks and legalized prostitution. It all sounded great, how could my life not get better there?

My first couple of months were spent hanging out with my family, going to casino after casino. A typical day for me would be spending the afternoon gambling, followed up by a giant casino buffet dinner. If you haven't been lucky enough to experience a Las Vegas buffet before, imagine yourself eating about 100,000 calories in one sitting. Within just a couple weeks, I began to notice I needed a bigger belt as my midsection grew. I had fun packing on the weight and losing my money on a daily basis, but I quickly became bored and began looking for a job.

I saw an advertisement for a job fair and went to check it out. I got my hair cut, wore my suit and sucked in my gut as I worked my way around the room. I stumbled onto a booth where a nice gentleman was offering jobs selling mobile homes. I wasn't interested in a job there, but I wanted to ask him why mobile home parks are always built in tornado prone areas. As we began talking, the conversation quickly changed from tornados to me taking a job working for his company.

Frankly, I wasn't the least bit interested in the job until he told me how much money I would be making. In an instant, my lack of interest in selling mobile homes was replaced by my desire for money. Before I knew it, I had just accepted a position as a salesman. I left the job fair with my sheet of new hire instructions so I could start that week. I felt like I was in a daze as I walked to my car in the parking lot, what did I just get myself into?

One of the first things I needed to do before starting work was to get a drug test. As I was driving to the testing facility, it began to sink in. A few short months ago I was a police officer and now here I was going to be selling mobile homes. I tried to convince myself that this was a lateral career move. I chuckled and wondered what the hell has happened to my life?

The more I thought about it, the more conflicted I became about my new job choice. Part of me was saying it was a great idea because I would be making good money. It would be nice to start having some money come in rather than deplete my savings by playing blackjack every day. The other part of me felt like I wasn't going to be happy. I struggled to find the pride in being a mobile home salesman. It was definitely not at the top of my list of dream jobs.

I figured I just needed to change my perception of the mobile homes. I had seen the units I would be selling and the truth is they were beautiful. In my mind, I tried to convince myself that they weren't mobile homes; they were state of the art modular residential units. They were modern marvels of contemporary living.

I was hoping that the semantics would change my perception of selling them. Unfortunately, it didn't work. I started to feel more anxiety about my decision to accept the position. Even though I didn't do drugs, I considered picking some up on the way in order to fail my drug test. This way I wouldn't have to continue struggling with my decision of taking the job, plus, I could hit up another buffet later and really pig out.

Even though I became more and more unsettled, I remained drug free on the way to the testing facility. After my drug test was over, I headed home and continued to try and convince myself that this job would be good for me. By the time I reached my apartment, I finally came to terms with the truth.

I didn't want to sell mobile homes. I was only interested in the job because of the money. In my past, I had traded my happiness for money. That was a terrible experience and I had promised myself I would never do that again. But here I was, ready to listen to my mind instead of my heart once again. I was angry that my mind almost took a job that I wasn't going to be happy at. I wanted to punch my mind right in the nose, or cerebral cortex, or something like that.

I was very glad that I was able to get in touch with my true feelings and not begin a path that could have taken my life a direction I didn't want to go. Thankfully I listened to my heart over my mind and made the right choice. It was very empowering to finally resist the urge to be practical over my desire to be happy. The good news is I went out for a great buffet that evening and then went shopping for a bigger belt.

It's Just Temporary

There is a strange thing that happens when we think situations will just be temporary, they often become permanent. Are there situations in your life that you thought were only going to be temporary, just for now, or until something better comes along? How long have you been stuck there?

The temporary situations that become permanent can happen in all areas of your life. It could be that you have lived in your "starter house" for 25 years. It could be that you will soon be retiring from your "temporary job" after 30 years of working there, or it could be that your "I'll just go out with them for now" relationship has just celebrated its 25th wedding anniversary.

I am not saying that those are all bad things, but it is bad if you haven't been happy in them for quite some time. You might look back and wonder how you have been there for such a long time, it was just supposed to be temporary. Time is a slippery thing. It is easy to be surprised at how quickly time passes.

It is important for you to be wary of telling yourself that a situation will just be temporary. The best way to avoid finding yourself stuck later on in your life in an unhappy situation is to prevent it from even starting. It is much easier to say no in the beginning than trying to change your situation later on. It reminds me of Nancy Reagan's anti-drug campaign from many years ago. The motto was "Just say no" to drugs. I think that is really good advice. I would also suggest to "Just say no" to situations that don't feel good from the very beginning.

Give Yourself A Happiness Checkup

Since time passes so quickly, it is important to periodically assess where you are in your life and see if what you have been doing is still making you happy. You can think of it as giving yourself a happiness review and checkup. Ask yourself how you are feeling about your current relationship, your living situation and your job. If you identify areas where you are not happy, it is important that you take action and make a change. If you don't, you will look back at some point in the future and regret not taking action when you had the chance.

Let me share a story with you of when I realized I was no longer happy at my job. What first started out as my dream job had turned into a nightmare. Luckily I was able to see that I needed to make a change and took action.

Escorted Out Of the Building

I was attending college and had a few more weeks before I would be finishing the Radiography Program. I planned on graduating and moving to California to live by the ocean. I figured I could shoot x-rays a couple days a week and then spend the rest of my time on the beach. I was ready to become the surfer boy that I always longed to be. I even began preparing by only buying t-shirts with pictures of waves on them.

My California dream looked like it was going to happen until I saw an ad for a management position that whet my appetite even more. The position was a PACS Administrator. The job consisted of managing the medical imaging system that the doctors and technologists used to import and diagnose patients' medical images.

Typically, an applicant would need 5 – 10 years of experience in the field to be considered for the position. Even though I had not even graduated from the Radiography Program yet, I wasn't going to let a little thing like having no experience prevent me from going for it. What I lacked in experience, I made up for with confidence and determination. The fact that I had a 4.0 GPA at the university and I received high marks at my clinical site also didn't hurt.

I interviewed for the position and got it. I was elated. Yay me! I graduated from the university and now began working for one of the most prestigious hospitals in Las Vegas. I was proud that my hard work had paid off and now I set myself up to have a bright future in medical imaging. It was a dream come true.

I loved my new job. My bosses were great and I liked my co-workers. The work was challenging at times, but I felt appreciated and valued. I received many letters of recognition and had high employee reviews. Things were going great for me. It looked like I was going to be happy there for a long time, then a funny thing happened.

As the years went on, I started to feel frustrated with the way things were being done. My workload was steadily increasing and it seemed like everything ended up being my responsibility. My requirement of being on call had increased from covering one hospital to covering five. I wouldn't have minded so much if I got paid to take call, but I did not. I was getting called at all hours of the day and night. I was miserable. It made me realize that being on call must be one of Dante's Seven Levels of Hell.

I tried to make changes and pitched several new ideas to upper management. I made fancy PowerPoint presentations that had elaborate graphics with many pie charts. Nothing demonstrates something is a good idea better than a presentation with lots of pie charts. I took one look at my boss and I could tell he was not impressed. Or perhaps he was very impressed and he just forgot to tell his face. Needless to say, my ideas did not get implemented.

I began to feel defeated and stuck. Why don't they understand my pain? Don't they know my ideas will solve everything, including global warming? I wondered if they forgot how valuable I was. I decided that if I was going to be unhappy at my job, then at the very least I deserved a raise.

I met with my boss and asked for a $10,000 raise. She looked as if she just found out she won a year's worth of baked beans instead of a Caribbean cruise on the TV game show "Let's Make a Deal". After about a minute, she regained her composure and said, "Wow, that's a lot of money." I held my ground and gave her all the reasons why I deserved such a raise. She said she would look into it and requested that I resubmit my resume for a salary review.

I honestly believed I would get the raise. I was good at what I did and I had very specialized knowledge. I thought my nearly 5 years' experience would make me invaluable to the company. I was wrong.

When my salary review was completed, I was told I was making exactly what I was supposed to be making, and no more. I thought that I might try to renegotiate. I considered downgrading my raise request to a couple hundred dollars or a Starbucks gift card, but at that point, I had a feeling I wasn't going to get those either.

I felt defeated and my personal life started to suffer. My feelings of hopelessness and powerlessness had creeped into my personal life. I felt tired all the time and I started saying no to invitations and just stayed at home. I was losing my sparkle as some people would say.

I was desperate to feel better in my situation. I tried everything I could think of to be happier. I tried meditating, chanting, and even began eating gluten free muffins, but nothing seemed to work. I was always worrying about work in the back of my mind. It seemed like even when I wasn't on call, I would be thinking about how long it was until I would have to be on call again.

I started to think about quitting my job. The thought of it was not pleasing. I had worked very hard to get where I was. I had almost 5 years' experience and couldn't bear the thought of throwing it all away. Maybe I just needed to look at my situation in a new way.

I started embracing several mantras to keep me from quitting my job. Statements like "There is no such thing as a perfect job", "There are politics in every organization", and "Company policies don't make sense anywhere." After several months of trying to convince myself I could find a way to be happy with my work situation, I came to the truth of the matter. Nothing was making me feel better and my heart was no longer in my job. It was time for me to leave.

I remember the morning I decided to give my 2 weeks' notice that I was quitting. I drove into work literally giddy with delight. I even let people cut in front of me at the highway merge ramp. I could barely wait to get to my work computer and fire off my resignation letter.

I went into my office and typed it out. My finger hesitated over the send button for a few minutes. I wondered if I was making the right decision. Was I sure about this? My job was not easy to come by and I would not be able to get a similar position any time soon. I closed my eyes, took a deep breath and hit the send button. I wondered what would happen next.

At just before noon, I got a call from my corporate boss who said he was in the building. He asked me if I could come meet him in the lobby. It was rare that he would come visit me on location. When I saw him in the lobby, he was not wearing his usual business casual clothes, he was wearing a suit. I knew then that it would be my last day.

I always got along well with him so there was no animosity or hard feelings. He knew I was unhappy at my job. We went back to my office and I handed over my laptop, cell phone and security cards. I gathered up all my personal belongings and said goodbye to my office. It was weird knowing I would not be working there any longer. I couldn't believe I quit. This is really happening.

My boss said he had to escort me out of the building. As we walked down the hall, it felt kind of weird. I didn't get fired and wasn't being removed for disciplinary reasons, why do I need an escort? I felt like if I was getting escorted out, maybe I should yell that this place sucks or at least kick over a garbage can on my way out. Besides, I could always use some more street cred.

I decided to play it cool and didn't cause a scene. When we came to the exit door, my boss and I shook hands and wished each other the best. I readjusted my cardboard box of belongings in my arms and opened the door. As soon as I stepped outside, the sunlight hit my face. Then something incredible happened.

It seemed as if the sun was shining a different color. It was more yellow and illuminating. I looked around and everything seemed more colorful and vibrant. The trees looked greener and every car that was in the parking lot looked like it had been freshly painted. I blinked my eyes several times and couldn't believe what I was seeing.

I know that sometimes people speak in metaphors or exaggerate to illustrate a point. But let me tell you something, I am not exaggerating in the least. The colors literally were brighter and more vibrant than I ever remembered them being. It was one of the most beautiful moments of my life.

I was nearly brought to tears seeing the bright colors all around me. I realized then that my heart had been suffering. It became clear that I had been missing out on much of life's joy by staying in a job I was not happy at. I was making a living but I wasn't living a life.

I was scared of what my future now held in store for me, but I knew I had made the right decision of quitting my job. My future was literally and figuratively brighter than ever before. It had taken me several months to finally listen to my heart, but I was no longer stuck and I knew there were going to be happier days ahead.

Forget The "Should"

Now let's talk about another reason why so many of us have difficulty being clear and comfortable with our desires. It is because there are so many outside influences trying to tell you who you should be and what you should want. These outside influences are all around you. They could be your parents, your family, your friends, your co-workers, the media, or even strangers. It is no wonder we can become confused and start doubting whether we know what is best for us.

It seems like the messages all around you are endless. You are constantly being told what kind of car you should drive, how much money you should make, and what kind of partner you should be with. The messages also try to shape and define your perception of what love, joy and success looks like.

Let me give you a quick example of how effective outside influences can be. If you have ever been married or engaged, chances are you were given a diamond ring. Did you ever wonder why a diamond is so symbolic of love? The reason is because the message was invented by De Beers Diamond Company in the 1940's to boost sales. Their advertising slogan "A diamond is forever" convinced everyone that a diamond is the most symbolic gesture of displaying your undying love for your partner. That is the simple reason why most people believe that giving your partner the biggest and nicest diamond you can buy is the best way to show your partner how much you love them.

It was the most successful marketing campaign ever created. It is amazing how powerful advertising can be and how it can influence our decisions and beliefs. On a side note, the original marketing plan was that a man should buy a diamond worth his annual salary instead of the two months' salary as is commonly accepted today. Can you imagine that?

Not only are the messages endless, they are also relentless. If you have ever had a parent tell you what you should do over and over again, then you know what I mean. It seems like every conversation begins and ends with all the things they think you should be doing. It is no wonder why we never answer the phone any more. Just kidding, your parents mean well.

The truth is outside influences are very powerful and can affect the choices and decisions you make for yourself. It is not surprising that we find ourselves in jobs that are prestigious by society's standards, but make us absolutely miserable. You might have lots of money, but still feel unsuccessful. You might be in a relationship with the man or woman of everyone else's dream, but not your own.

We have given too much credibility to those who think they know what is best for us. It is time for you to take back your personal power and realize that nobody knows you better than you. Nobody has walked in your shoes. Nobody knows what makes you laugh, smile, or makes you cry. How could it be that someone else could possibly know what is going to bring you the most joy?

Remember, it is your life and you have the freedom to choose what your life will become. Don't be afraid to go against what others say you should be or do. Be bold and courageous in your decisions. It's great to take advice from people, but never let their opinion be the deciding vote on which direction you should take. Never give up your freedom to choose your own destiny.

The Power Of Visualizing

Having a clear vision of what you want is vital to living the life of your dreams, but sometimes it can be hard to know what options to choose. Many people have difficulty knowing what they want because they have never experienced it before. How could you know if you like something if it has not even happened yet? Luckily, visualizing is an amazing process you can use to help you answer those questions.

Visualizing is a valuable tool to help you assess what you want and who you want to be. Even though there are many things you have never done or experienced, visualizing can generate the feelings as if you had. The feelings that you get from imagining yourself doing something will give you a good idea what the experience would actually be like in real life.

Visualizing is an excellent tool to experiment with all the possibilities in your life. You can imagine different partners, different jobs, and different places to live. You can imagine anything and everything that you might desire. The feelings you experience will help guide you to making the right decisions about which direction you should head.

You Have To Feel Something

The most important aspect of visualizing is you must get an emotional feeling when you are using your imagination. It is not enough just to think about something and picture it; you need to be able to generate an emotional reaction to what you are seeing in your mind. If you are thinking about something and not getting an emotional feeling, you are just daydreaming.

There is a big difference between visualizing and daydreaming. Daydreaming is using your imagination to kill time or mentally escape for a few minutes. When you visualize, you are doing it with purpose and intention. Your intention is to see how something feels that you would like to consider experiencing in real life.

When you begin to visualize with purpose, you will create scenarios in your mind that will help you develop emotions as if the situation is real and not just your imagination. The feelings you get from your visualizations will help you determine what life choices could bring you the most joy.

There Are No Limits

There are no limits to what you can visualize. You can be, do, and say anything you can imagine. It is like going window shopping in your mind. You can imagine yourself being a waiter, a doctor, or a teacher. You can picture yourself being married with children, or being single and partying up a storm. You can imagine yourself living by the beach or living in the mountains. There are endless things you can imagine yourself doing and being. Just like in real life, have fun exploring all the wonderful opportunities to live the life of your dreams.

Make The Visualization As Real As Possible

The best way to generate emotions is to make your visualization as real as possible. Use your imagination to add details to what you see in your mind. Think of how things look, how they smell, how they taste, and how they feel on your skin. See yourself responding to the people and places in your visualization.

The more detailed and realistic your visualization is, the more emotions you will be able to generate. You can add or remove any details you want. You can fine tune your visualization to suit your desires. Once you allow yourself the freedom to experiment, you'll be surprised at how easy it will be to generate an emotion for what you are visualizing.

Allow your visualizations to go as far as you desire. Once you are done visualizing, it is helpful to write down what scenarios gave you the best feelings. Write down the key elements from the scenarios that made you feel good. You can now look for these elements in the real world and make your visualizations a reality.

Chapter Summary

- You can be anything and do anything you desire

- You need to know what the life of your dreams looks like

- Your heart is the best tool to help you find the right path for your life

- Be wary of temporary things becoming permanent

- Do not let other people determine what your life will be

- Use visualization to help you reveal what will make you happy

Action Plan

What does your Big Juicy Life look like?

Write a few sentences about what you want in each category. Make sure you do not rationalize or minimize your true desires. Go big! Remember, it is your life and you can have it all.

Job/Career

_____

_____

_____

_____

Romantic Relationship

_____

_____

_____

_____

Friends

_____

_____

_____

_____

Activities/Hobbies

_____

_____

_____

_____

Travel/Vacation

_____

_____

_____

_____

Lifestyle

_____

_____

_____

_____

Money

_____

_____

_____

_____

Giving Back To Others

_____

_____

_____

_____

Family

_____

_____

_____

_____

Add Your Own Category (_____)

_____

_____

_____

_____

Add Your Own Category (_____)

_____

_____

_____

_____

Did you have any difficulty in being honest with yourself about what you truly desire? Take a minute and review what you wrote down. I want you to make sure that your desires are your own, and not from an outside source or influence. Make sure your desires are not what you think you should want, but what your heart truly wants. Make any changes necessary to your categories.

Visualize to help you see what you might like.

If you are not sure of what you want in certain categories, begin to visualize different possibilities to see which ones feel good. Remember to have fun and allow yourself the ultimate freedom to imagine anything and everything you might desire. Use these steps to get the most out of your visualizations.

Step 1. Determine what possibilities you would like to "try on".

Step 2. Begin visualizing. Make the situation as detailed as possible. Allow yourself to start believing the visualization is real. Be aware of what emotions you develop from each scenario that you imagine.

Example: See yourself in your dream job. What are you doing? Who are you working with? What is your work environment? What type of clothing are you wearing? Create the details for all these different elements in your mind. The more detailed it is, the easier it will be to generate an emotion from it.

Step 3. Write down the key elements of your visualization that made you feel good.

Example: It felt good to work outdoors.

1. _____

2. _____

3. _____

4. _____

Now you can use these elements to begin making better choices that are in alignment with what you are truly longing for. When you begin to look at new opportunities, you can see if they have the key elements that you discovered make you feel good.

Daily Action:

1. As you go about your daily life, allow yourself the freedom to imagine different possibilities of what might make you happy. You might talk to someone about their position and think that it sounds appealing. Visualize yourself in their job and see how it feels. You can do this with jobs, partners, activities, etc. It will open your mind to new possibilities for love, joy and success that you have not considered before.

2. Take the word "should" out of your vocabulary. When you stop saying "should" to other people, you are giving people more freedom to live their heart's desires. In life, whatever we give to others, we ultimately also give to ourselves. When you stop saying "should" to others, you are also taking away the power of anyone else's influence when they say "should" to you. This simple step will help you break free from the heaviness of feeling like you have to conform to others beliefs.

3. Words are very powerful. There are better ways of offering advice to other people rather than saying "should". You can say "you might want to consider", or "a good idea might be to". These phrases feel better to the person and makes them feel like they have choices. It makes them feel that they get to decide and their decision is not being determined for them. Try it and see what a better response you get from people.

"It is not death that a man should fear, but he should fear
never beginning to live."

- **Marcus Aurelius**

Chapter 4: Live Like You Were Dying

Let me ask you a question. What are some of your
dreams and desires that you are hoping to experience in the
future? Maybe it is a trip to an exotic destination, starting
your own business, or falling in love again. Have you been
taking consistent action in making those dreams a reality or
have you been procrastinating?

For many of us, we feel like we have an endless supply of
time to do everything we want. This feeling allows us to be
complacent and not have any sense of urgency about taking
action. Many people put things off and say, "I will do it
tomorrow". When tomorrow comes, they put it off again and
say "I will do it tomorrow". This pattern repeats itself until
one day, they have run out of time.

The truth is time passes by quickly, and it is important to
understand that you do have a limited time on this earth.
Even though we are all limited in time, do not let that scare
you. The value and fulfillment of one's life is not based on
the amount of time you have; it is based on what you have
done with that time.

Life is meant to be lived to its fullest. In order to do that,
you need to make the most of your time. It is important that
you have a clear vision of what you want and consistently
take action towards making it a reality. If you have difficulty

in being focused and energized, what would it take for you to change your lifestyle and stop procrastinating?

Many times, people are only spurred into action by experiencing tragedy or a near death experience. When that happens, suddenly they see the world with fresh eyes and a newfound sense of purpose, direction and most importantly, a sense of urgency. It is amazing how an unexpected situation can make you see how precious time really is.

In this chapter, I will motivate you to take action without having a near-death experience or having to go through some type of tragedy. I will show you how to live in the moment and allow yourself to see what is truly important in your life. You will learn to be bold in your decision making and be comfortable taking risks. I will show you how to make the most of ALL your time.

First, let me share a story with you that changed my life forever. I had always felt like a lack of time would never be an issue for me. I was young, strong and virile. I felt invincible and wasn't afraid of dying, that is something that happens to old people, not me. I never even considered that I would not have enough time to do all the things I dreamt of. I had a very rude awakening that made me see how precious time really is.

I Am Too Young To Die

I had gotten hired as a bartender at a new fine dining restaurant on the famous Las Vegas strip. The restaurant had the best filet mignon in town and live jazz music every evening. It had beautiful gold curtains inside and a glass enclosed wine room. I was thrilled to begin working at this amazing restaurant. The restaurant was opening soon, and we were in the final stages of our training.

One evening, I came home from work and began feeling ill. I felt weak and my body was a little achy. I thought my immune system might be drained due to the long hours of the restaurant training program and I might have caught a cold. I didn't think it was a big deal though. I knew it would be no match for the licorice flavored nighttime cold medicine that had never let me down before.

After I downed a shot of the medicine, I eagerly waited for the effects to kick in. After several minutes, I was surprised that I wasn't feeling better. In fact, I was feeling worse. I felt weaker than before and now I was experiencing a sensation of pressure on my chest.

I waited another 15 minutes to see if the medicine was going to take effect. It didn't. I began to wonder what the heck was going on with me. The pressure on my chest kept increasing and I became more concerned. I had the symptoms of having a heart attack, but I thought I was too young and healthy for that.

I battled with myself over whether or not I should go to the hospital. I did not want to overreact, it was probably nothing. I then remembered that many men die because they wait too long before they get medical help. You know, that male macho type personality. I decided it would be better to play it safe and look like a wimp rather than be a dead macho man.

I called 911 and told the operator that I thought I was having a heart attack. The ambulance came and took me to the hospital. As soon as I arrived, the pokes and prods began immediately. It seemed like they were drawing more blood from me than I had ever given in my lifetime. I was feeling weaker by the moment and offered no resistance to the numerous needle stings.

As I listened to the chirps and beeps of the monitors I was hooked up to, I tried to figure out what was wrong with me. Maybe I had the flu, food poisoning or maybe a respiratory infection. An hour later, a doctor approached me and told me the news I had feared the most. I had a heart attack.

Suddenly, it felt like everything went into slow motion. It seemed like the doctor was speaking in low drawn out words. I tried hard to concentrate on every word he was saying, but all I could comprehend was I would be scheduled to have an angioplasty. I had so many questions but was unable to mouth the words in time, and in a moment he was gone.

I laid there in complete shock and disbelief that this was happening to me. It didn't make any sense. I was 36 years old and in great shape. No one in my family had a history of heart trouble. I had great blood pressure and had no risk factors for heart disease. Hell, I had never even smoked a cigarette in my life. How can this be possible?

After a few minutes, my shock turned into fear. I wondered if I was going to die. Is this how it ends for me? I started thinking about all the things I had not done or experienced yet. I wanted to have children, I wanted to learn to play the guitar, and I wanted to go to Italy. It seemed like so many things I had been putting off were popping into my mind.

I began feeling sad about all the things I never got a chance to do. Why didn't I do those things when I had the time? A sense of frustration came over me. I had wasted so much time and now it looked like my life was over. I wanted more time, wait, I don't want more time, I need more time! I am too young to die!

The rest of the night was spent going over my life and thinking of all the things I would do if I had more time. I fell asleep wondering if I would live through the night or possibly die from the angioplasty procedure that was scheduled for the next day.

The next morning I was awoken from my sleep by a loud commotion. There was shouting all over in the emergency room. Everyone was moving frantically and I could not figure out what was going on. I saw several people pointing to the TV in the middle of the room. I looked up to see what all the excitement was about. I watched in horror as I saw a plane fly into one of the towers of the World Trade Center.

Suddenly I realized I must be dreaming. It all started to make sense now. My heart attack and the plane flying into the World Trade Center is just my imagination running amok while I am sleeping. I better stop eating those burritos before I go to bed. I took a deep breath and allowed myself to relax for a moment. This will all be over soon I thought. I will wake up and be in my bed all comfy and warm.

After a few seconds, I realized I was still stuck in this terrible dream. I pinched my arm to wake myself up. It didn't work. I pinched myself as hard as I could, but nothing changed. I held my breath until I became dizzy, but I was still stuck in this nightmare. I became frantic and shook my head violently. I screamed to myself, Wake up! Wake up!

I tried everything I could think of but nothing awoke me from this nightmare. I realized this wasn't a dream after all, this was reality. I slowly tried to come to terms with what was happening. It was difficult to comprehend that this was all real. Not only was my life in jeopardy at 36 years old, but two planes had just brought down the World Trade Center.

I tried to stay calm and focus on what was happening with me in the hospital. I still couldn't wrap my head around the fact that I had a heart attack. I didn't care what the doctor said, it made no sense. As I was being prepped for my angioplasty procedure, a nurse came and asked me to sign the consent form. I told her I was having doubts that I actually had a heart attack and was thinking about refusing the procedure. She sent my doctor over to speak with me. I told him maybe I had the flu or some type of virus. He became angry and said "No! You had a heart attack. You need to have this procedure or you could die."

Even though he might have been right, I still thought he was wrong. I was sure they would not find any blockages in my heart. Besides that, I was also afraid the angioplasty might kill me and they would later find out I didn't have a heart attack after all. I decided I was willing to take the chance that I might die if I didn't have the procedure. All I wanted to do was go home and curl up with my dog in my arms. If I was going to die, that is where I wanted to be.

I refused the procedure and was signed out of the hospital AMA (Against Medical Advice). My father picked me up and drove me home. I was still so weak, I could barely sit upright. As we were driving, I felt like a rag doll swaying into the passenger door with each turn around a corner.

On the way home, my father stopped by a restaurant to pick up some food for me. As we pulled into the parking lot, I saw a girl I recently wanted to ask out on a date. She was walking into the restaurant with a friend; both were laughing and smiling. It felt like I was watching a movie.

It was a cruel example of what possibilities for happiness I would no longer have. I sat there helpless, watching the last glimpse into what my life had been. It wasn't fair that I didn't get a full life. I felt like I wanted a do-over. There was still so much I hadn't done. I thought of how I would do things differently if I had more time.

My next few days were spent lying in my bed with my dog curled up next to me. I was scared every time I went to sleep, wondering if I would wake up or die during the evening. As more time passed, I began feeling stronger and stronger. I eventually fully recovered from my cardiac episode, but that experience changed my life forever.

It made me look at my life and see areas where I was not living life to the fullest. I decided I would stop procrastinating and begin to take more action to make my dreams become reality. I would be bolder in pursuing my desires and not wait until tomorrow to make things happen. I had a newfound sense and appreciation of my limited time and I wasn't going to waste any of it.

The experience also made me see where I was making my life harder than it needed to be. I was a chronic worrier from the time I was a child. I would obsess over making the right decisions at all times. I was good at judging myself harshly and carrying around a lot of guilt and regret at the pain I caused others and myself. I decided I did not want to continue living that way

I no longer wanted to sweat the details of life and be such a worrier. I wanted to live a more carefree life. I wanted to be more forgiving of others and myself. I was determined to let go of the past and appreciate each moment of my life more. I strived to fully concentrate on being present at all times and embrace the here and now. I realized the joy of life is only available in the present moment.

My heart attack had opened my eyes in so many different ways, but I was not the only one who had a life changing experience on September 11. The attack on the World Trade Center thrust our country into doubt and confusion. It did not change the belief in our country's resilience, but it shook many people's feelings of stability and sense that there would always be enough time.

The attack on September 11 was a wakeup call to people who were just going through their everyday life without any sense of urgency. It destroyed the illusion that there will always be a tomorrow. People began to look at their lives like never before. Many people realized they were taking life, people and time for granted. New perceptions of what is truly important in life began being solidified.

After that infamous day, families began holding each other tighter and "I love you" flowed more frequently than ever before. There was a deeper appreciation of all the little things around us that suddenly seemed so much more valuable. People began making better use of their time, and began filling each moment with more love and happiness.

If you lived through the aftermath of September 11, you undoubtedly have a story about what an impact it made on the way you see your life and what is important to you. It is often through tragedy and hardships that we can gain the most clarity on who we are and what we want out of life. The good news is you do not need to have a near-death experience or tragedy to live with more intention, motivation and happiness. All you need is a change in mindset.

Stop Procrastinating

Most of us have big plans for our lives. There is so much we want to be, do and see in our lifetime. So why is it that so many of us never really go after our dreams? What are you waiting for? Procrastination can make you miss out on so much love, joy and success in your life.

It is time for you to shake off the rust, get energized, and take action. I am not saying that you have to go skydiving this afternoon, but I am suggesting you stop for a moment and take a look at what your dreams and desires are. Have you been taking consistent action in making them reality? Think about things that you have said that you will do next week, next month or next year. Why not do them sooner? Do they really have to wait?

The Perfect Time

There are many reasons why people procrastinate. One of the biggest reasons is people tend to wait until the "perfect time" arrives. They are convinced that they need to wait to take action until they are older, lose weight, have more money, or some other arbitrary factor. They convince themselves that the timing is off and they must postpone taking action to a later date. It is one of the biggest mistakes that people make.

The truth is there is no such thing as a "perfect time." If you wait for the perfect time, you will be waiting forever. Before you know it, you will go from waiting for the perfect time to realizing you have missed your opportunity. Instead of worrying about trying to time life perfectly, be more concerned about running out of time and never taking the chance to make all of your dreams come true. Think about this example; if you were a player on a basketball court, you do not want to be still holding the ball when the buzzer sounds. Keep taking shots until there is no more time left.

Let Go Of Your Ego

There are many reasons why people do not go after their dreams. One of the biggest reasons is a fear of judgment from other people. What will people say if my business fails? Will people laugh at me if they find out I got rejected? What if people think my book idea is stupid? It is when you start to imagine all the things that could go wrong that your ego steps in and tells you it is best that you do not even try. You should play it safe and not take the chance of being hurt.

The ego has good intentions, but by trying to keep you safe all the time, you never have a chance to succeed. You have to take risks if you are going to be successful. It is like first learning to ride a bicycle. You start out with training wheels attached to your bike to keep you from falling over and getting hurt. Over time, you become bored and you are longing for the thrill of riding on just two wheels. One day, you become brave and take off the training wheels.

Your heart starts pounding and you are scared you might fall, but you are determined to make it happen. You take a deep breath, grip the handlebars tightly and start pedaling as fast as you can. Your bike wobbles for a few feet and then all of a sudden you find the balance between you and the bike. You go sailing down the block smiling and laughing. There is no stopping you now!

You must overcome your fear of failing in order to take advantage of all the endless opportunities for love, joy and success. If you are too afraid of failing and worrying about what people might say, you will miss out on so much happiness. You don't want to be stuck on the bike with the training wheels all your life, do you?

Now let me tell you a little secret that might just change the way you look at your fear of being judged. The secret is "People are going to talk about you no matter what." It does not matter even if you are the most successful, the most knowledgeable, or the best-looking person in the room. No one is safe from ridicule or comments. That might sound like a sad statement, but it is very freeing once you accept it as a normal part of life. It is quite liberating when you realize that even if your ego protects you from any actions that might be seen negatively by others, people will still talk about you and make judgments.

Once you let go of your desire to be seen in the perfect light, you can begin to take risks and chase your dreams. You will feel much lighter when you stop trying to micromanage every interaction with every person, even strangers. It is time to tap into your freedom and realize that the best use of your time is always spent by striving to find your own happiness and not worry what other people might think of you. Who cares what they think, go have fun.

Have you ever seen someone who is a terrible dancer having the time of their life on the dance floor? They are laughing and smiling, and it seems like they do not care who is watching. There might be people who are standing off to the side and making rude comments about the dancer. The big question is who made the best use of their time? Was it the person dancing and having fun, or the people standing around doing the judging?

Grandparent Exercise

I am going to ask you to do a quick little exercise right now. I would like you to choose one of your grandparents and make a list of everything you know about him or her. Choose the grandparent you know the most about. They could be living or deceased.

You can start with generalities that you know about them, like where did they live, what they did for a living, etc. Then begin to get more detailed. Write down some of their biggest accomplishments, their most significant failures, and their biggest dreams and regrets. Write down everything you know about them. Feel free to use another sheet of paper if necessary. Take a few minutes and complete your list.

Write down everything you know about your grandparent.

1. _____

2. _____

3. _____

4. _____

5. _____

6. _____

7. _____

8. _____

9. _____

10. _____

11. _____

12. _____

13. _____

14. _____

15. _____

16. _____

Now take a look at your list. Were you surprised at how little you knew about your grandparent? Were most of the details on your list just generalities about their lives? Did you know many specific details about their biggest accomplishments, regrets and failures?

If your list was quite short or even empty, do not feel bad. I have done this exercise with many people and most times, the list is quite short. If you did know a lot about your grandparent, that is wonderful. How cool is it to know the personal side of the people in your family lineage.

This exercise illustrates several things. The most important thing is a significant amount of information about our lives is not passed down from generation to generation. For most people, there is very little known about their grandparents. Let's expand it a bit and see what you know about your great-grandparents, I bet it is even less information. If people in their own family lineage don't know much about their ancestors from just forty to sixty years ago, what does that say about how people are going to remember the details of your life?

In 100 Years, It Won't Matter

The truth is, in 100 years, the chances are good that no one is going to remember the details of your life. More importantly, people will not remember what your failures were. In 100 years, there will be nobody left to tell the embarrassing story about when your big idea of opening up a drive-thru pizzeria failed. There will not be a monument erected to memorialize the time you failed to make the team. School children will not be told the story about how you got rejected when you asked out the hot guy or girl for a date.

The point is that we can be very egocentric in our lives. Many of us believe that people are talking about us and chronicling our every success and failure. We incorrectly believe that our mistakes and failures will haunt us for the rest of our lives and maybe even beyond that. Nothing could be further from the truth.

It is amazingly liberating to understand that in the grand scheme of things, it doesn't really matter what you do. Nobody is going to remember, and even if they do remember, nobody is going to care. Do not think of that as a bad thing, think of it as ultimate freedom.

There is nothing to fear anymore when you realize all this is just temporary. It is time to give the green light to all your dreams and desires. It's time to embrace your freedom and take advantage of all the wonderful opportunities you have to make all your dreams come true. And remember; always get on the dance floor every chance you get. It's wonderful that nobody is going to remember how bad you danced, but what you will remember is all the fun you had. That is what life is all about.

Live Like A Fruit Fly

By now, hopefully you have realized the importance of making the most of your time and taking action now. I am going to give you one more inspirational example. Did you know that a fruit fly only lives for 48 hours? Do you think he is worried about rejection? Do you think he is going to care what other fruit flies might say about him?

We might look at that fruit fly and feel a sense of sadness. We might say poor Mr. Fruit Fly, he only has 48 hours to live. I hope he makes the most of his time and fills his short life with all the happiness he can find. I am glad I am not a fruit fly.

In the same sense, a cosmic being that lives for 5,000 years might look at us and say poor humans, you only have 100 years to live. That doesn't seem like a lot of time to do a lot of things. I hope they make the most of the short time that they have. I am glad I am not a human.

Time is relative. What a long time means to someone may be considered a short time to another. The key is to make the most of whatever time you have and make it the most enjoyable that it can possibly be. The best way to do that is to always live in the present moment.

When we are focused on the past or worrying about the future, we are missing out on the happiness that is available to us now. The gifts of life are always in the present. That is really the only place you can have any affect anyway. You cannot change your past and you cannot live in the future. When striving for more happiness, success and love, always concentrate on what you can do at this moment, right now, to make your life more enjoyable.

Chapter Summary

- Your time is limited

- It is not the amount of time you have that is most important, it is what you do with that time that is most important

- There is no such thing as the "Perfect Time" to take action

- In 100 years, nobody is going to remember or care about what you did in your life

- Be bold in chasing all your dreams

- Take consistent action

- Make the most of your life by living in the present moment and not in the past or future

Action Plan

Make a list of things you would like to do before you die. Many people call it a bucket list. You don't need to call it a bucket list, you can give it a more fun name. You can call it your "YOLO" list. (YOLO means You Only Live Once). Or perhaps you could personalize it with your name. If your name is Diane, you can call it Diane's Daring and Delightful Desires.

Example: Go skydiving.

1. _____

2. _____

3. _____

4. _____

5. _____

6. _____

7. _____

8. _____

9. _____

10. _____

Now commit to start checking off things on your list!

Be sure to include some easily done items so you will gain momentum and feel the joy of checking things off your list. The ability to accomplish even small items on your list will give you an immense feeling of happiness, control, and the belief that you can live the life of your dreams.

Taking action is not only about doing new things, it is also about stopping things that do not serve you. Make a list of things you will commit to stopping within a certain time frame. When you decide on what your time frame is, commit to accomplishing your goal within that time period. Remember, don't put off things. If they can be done sooner, then do it.

Example: I am going to stop smoking within 4 months.

1. _____

2. _____

3. _____

4. _____

5. _____

Congratulations on taking action to make your life better!

"To Do Lists" can help you prioritize your time and make the best use of it. Instead of running through all the things you need to do over and over again in your mind, you will have them all down on paper. You can then focus on taking action on completing them rather wasting time worrying about them.

Make a "To Do List" of tasks you would like to accomplish this weekend. You can include some things you might have been putting off or have been weighing on your mind.

Example: I am going to replace all the burned out lightbulbs in the whole house.

1. _____

2. _____

3. _____

4. _____

5. _____

Were you surprised at how many things you were able to check off your list? Did you make better use of your time by having your desires written down? If this was helpful to you, you can begin using "To Do Lists" on a frequent basis. You can make them daily, weekly, monthly or any other time frame you desire.

Daily Action:

1. Do not procrastinate. Take consistent daily action towards making your dreams and goals become reality. Baby steps are all it takes to make big things happen. Think about this, you can literally walk from New York to California; you just need to walk each day. There is no way you could fail. Do not underestimate the power of taking consistent small steps when you are headed in the right direction.

2. Be bold in trying to make your dreams become reality. Even if they do not work as well as you hoped for, you will never have to live with the regret of not trying at all. It is better to have tried and failed rather than wondering if you would have been successful.

3. When you feel yourself getting upset about things, see if they are really worth wasting your time over. They might be small things like being cut off in traffic, reacting to an offhanded comment from a friend or colleague, or feeling slighted by a stranger. Remember, each minute you spend being angry or unhappy is one less minute you could have filled with joy. Start to let things go quicker and easier.

"Ask the right questions if you're going to find the right answers."

- Vanessa Redgrave

Chapter 5: Becoming Your Own Guru

Have you ever hoped to find a mystical guru who could give you the answers to all your biggest questions? Have you ever pictured yourself traveling to a faraway land in pursuit of a guru's knowledge? Can you see yourself climbing a mountain staircase into the clouds and finally entering the monastery where the guru resides? What would you ask him or her?

Instead of searching for a guru, maybe you have spent money on past life regressions, psychics and crystal balls. Or perhaps you have based your biggest life decisions on what your friends and family members recommend. All of this can be valuable to help guide you on your path, but wouldn't it be great if you could just have someone who's always around and would be the best person to guide you in your life?

I have great news for you! You already have someone who is very close to you who knows all the answers to your questions. This person will amaze you with their insight and accuracy. It is uncanny how they always seem to know exactly what you are thinking.

This person can go by many names; guru, sage, or all-knowing enlightened being. But the name you probably know them best by is "YOU". It is ironic that so often we look outside of ourselves to find answers to questions regarding us. The truth is nobody knows what's best for you, than you.

In this chapter, I'm going to show you how to become your own guru. It is very easy and the great news is that you are always accessible. There is no need to set an appointment, worry about fees, or save enough money to travel half way around the world to speak with the mystical guru.

You will also learn how to tap into your own mind and emotions, which will guide you better than anyone else ever could. You will find knowledge within that you didn't even know existed. You will develop more trust and belief in your own knowledge than ever before.

Now I am going to give you the three keys to becoming your own guru. The first one is to understand the amazing power of asking yourself questions. The second one is to make sure you are asking the right questions. The third key is to build trust and faith that you know what's best for you rather than anyone else.

Once you embrace your ability to become your own guru, there is no problem you cannot solve or situation where you will feel stuck. You can harness your innate wisdom for answers to things you have never even experienced before. Let me share a story with you about how I was able to tap into my own hidden knowledge and help someone in need.

But How Can I Help

I had been living in Las Vegas for 6 years and had changed jobs several times. It was not because I got fired I assure you, it was just because I was always looking for the next job that seemed more fun. I decided I was ready to settle down job wise and started looking for a new career.

I had always been interested in the human body and I liked science. I thought the medical field would be perfect for me. I checked into several medical programs and decided to apply to the Radiography Program at the University of Nevada, Las Vegas. It was a selective program and I was thrilled I was accepted.

I was determined to do my very best and make the most of this new learning opportunity. I asked myself how I could get more involved with the program and my fellow students. I decided to run for president of our student organization. I hadn't been a class president since the fourth grade, but luckily I was elected to be the new president.

Part of our organization's goal was to help support the students in any way possible, focusing mainly on academic tutoring. We were also a social group that supported each other outside of classes. I learned there was a classmate named Heidi who had Ewing's Sarcoma. Ewing's Sarcoma is a rare form of cancer that is often deadly. Heidi was just 22 years old.

I was doing my clinical internship at the same hospital as Heidi. I got the opportunity to see what a wonderful person she was. She could light up the room with her big blue eyes, blond hair and beautiful smile. She was smart, kind, and dedicated to her studies. We talked from time to time and she shared with me her personal battle with cancer. I learned that her cancer treatment was quite expensive and the financial burden was very stressful for her and her family.

I thought how helpful it would be if our student organization could help raise money to assist with her medical care. I had a deep desire to help her and a strong belief that somehow I could. I remember the day I walked up to her in the hospital and told her I was going to launch a charity on her behalf. I told her I'm not just going to raise dollars for you, I'm going to raise THOUSANDS of dollars for you.

I don't know where those words came from. They just seemed to slip out of my mouth. I walked away shocked with what I just promised her. I had never done any fundraising before. I couldn't even run a successful lemonade stand and now I just committed myself to raising thousands of dollars.

Luckily, I was not alone in my desire to help Heidi. There were many other people that also wanted to help. One of them was the Radiography Program Director Dr. George Pales. Dr. Pales is a wonderful and compassionate man who always strived to help students in any way possible. I met with him and told him of my desire to start a charity to raise money for Heidi's medical care. He thought it was a great idea and wanted to be a big part of it.

Together we founded a fundraising organization called Help Heidi. Neither of us had any real experience in fundraising. We both wondered where do we even start. There were so many questions of how we were going to make it successful. We had to figure out how we were going to raise money, who wanted to help, how could we get community support, how could we get national exposure, how were we going to keep track of the money, and how could we support Heidi in other ways? There were times when it seemed like it was not possible to find the answers to put it all together and make it work.

The good news is we never gave up. We found great answers to all our questions and the charity was a huge success. We raised over $33,000 to assist Heidi with her medical care. It was amazing to see how well everything came together in the end. In hindsight, I realized it was so successful because everyone involved had believed that it could be done and that together, we would find the answers to make it work.

Working with Dr. Pales and founding that charity is one of the best things I have ever done in my life. It showed me that I could make a difference in someone's life even when I was unsure of all the details. Many times we stop ourselves from getting involved because we feel like we are not the right person or do not have the skills or knowledge to help out. That could not be further from the truth. You are the right person to do it and you will find the answers to make it work. You CAN make a difference.

The great news is that Heidi beat her cancer. She completed the Radiography Program and went on to become a successful chiropractor. She is married and has two wonderful children.

The Power Of Asking Yourself Questions

The human brain is the most knowledgeable supercomputer that there is, or ever will be. Our brains are miracles of infinite magnitude. How can a few pounds of organic material provide so much wisdom and insight?

One of the great things our minds can do is find answers to any question we ask it. Let me give you a quick example of your amazing brainpower. Ask yourself what is 9 times 9. If you did not get 81, please put this book down and kindly report back to the third grade. The brain can easily handle simple questions like the above math problem, but it can also answer deeper and more complex questions.

On a personal level, our brains help guide us in making the right choices, everything from what should I do with my life to what should I have for lunch. It is quite impressive how efficient your brain is at finding answers and solutions. The good news is your mind never takes a day off, it is always there just waiting for you to ask it something. I think your mind deserves a raise.

Your Brain Has No Filter

As amazing as the mind is, it works quite mechanically at its core. It will only find answers to the questions you ask of it. The mind does not judge what questions you ask, it just looks for the answers to your questions. For example, if I ask myself "Why don't people like me?" my brain does not refuse to answer it, it will find an answer.

It would be great if the mind filtered out questions we asked of it. Can you imagine if your brain would refuse to answer questions that are not in your best interest? If you asked it "Why don't people like me?" it would give you a warning and say "I am not going to allow that question because it does not serve you. I suggest you ask me why are you so wonderful." Think how much better we would all feel about ourselves; we would no longer need anti-depressants, psychiatrists or Facebook.

Ask Yourself Better Questions

You have always had this amazing ability to find answers to questions in your life, but chances are you have not been making the best use of it. There are several mistakes many people make that do not allow your brain to give you the help it can. The biggest mistake is we ask ourselves lousy questions. We set ourselves up for fear, doubt and pain by asking questions that are not helpful.

If I ask myself "Why am I a bad person?" my mind will begin working on answering that question. It will look back in my life's history and find examples of when I lied, cheated, or stolen; hypothetically of course. Now all of those statements may be true, but they don't reflect the full picture of who I am. If I keep asking myself lousy questions, I will feel pretty crummy about myself. And that is exactly what many people do, they just keep asking themselves bad questions.

When you start asking yourself better questions, you will start feeling better and more positive. Let me give you an example. If I ask myself "Why am I a good person?" my brain will find answers to that also. It will find examples of when I was compassionate, loving, and generous. Those answers will make you feel better about yourself rather than the answers to the negative questions.

You might be wondering how it is possible that we can find reasons why we are both a good person and a bad person. The truth is we have experiences that would fit into a wide range of judgements, both good and bad. There are many different experiences and reasons why you can see yourself in different ways. Unfortunately though, we tend to concentrate and focus on the negative aspects of ourselves rather than the positive.

When you ask questions of yourself, choose ones that will make you feel good. Pick questions that will make you motivated, optimistic and happy. There is no need to ask lousy questions that will guarantee answers which will make you feel bad about yourself.

Don't Ask Negative Leading Questions

It is very important that you are aware of how you are wording questions to yourself. You never want to ask yourself negative leading questions. A negative leading question is a question where you are already assuming something bad. For example, a negative leading question would be asking yourself "Why don't people like me?" You are already assuming that people don't like you. You will find answers why that belief is true. What possible good could come from looking for proof that people don't like you?

You might be surprised at how many negative questions you ask yourself. Take a moment and see if you normally phrase your questions in a negative or in a positive way. It is easy to beat yourself up with bad questions, but it is even easier to build yourself up with good ones. When you catch yourself asking negative questions, stop and flip them to positive ones.

It is easy to flip a negative question into a positive one. Instead of asking yourself "Why don't people like me?" ask yourself "Why do people like me?" The information you get from both questions will feel true, but which answers will give you more helpful information and make you feel happier?

It might be hard to find positive questions when you have made a mistake or done something wrong. You don't have to avoid reality or deny the truth of what happened, but instead of asking yourself how you could have been so stupid, ask yourself more positive and helpful questions.

Concentrate on finding the good that can come from something bad. Ask yourself what you can do to make sure that it doesn't happen again? Ask yourself what was the positive lesson you learned from making that mistake? These questions will allow you to focus on your growth and moving forward and not staying behind and feeling more pain.

Believe That You Know Best

Many of us look for answers outside of ourselves. There is nothing wrong with that, but it seems like we have placed ourselves toward the bottom of the knowledge scale. Why is it that we think the janitor at work will have the best relationship advice for us, the waiter at the restaurant will know what stocks we should buy, or a stranger at the bus stop will know what we should do with our lives?

The biggest reason we look outside of ourselves is that we don't believe that we know what's best for us. You can be swayed by outside influences all around you that can be quite convincing. These ideas could come from family, friends, peers, media, etc. It seems like so many other people are so clear on what you should do.

Have you ever had the experience of being quite sure of what you wanted to do, and then someone says you should do something different. All of a sudden, you start second guessing yourself and doubting your decision. You might start thinking that they know what's best for you and end up doing what they suggest instead of what you had planned on.

It is great that you use other people's opinions and advice to help you with your decisions, but don't let anyone make the final decision for you. You need to have trust in your own knowledge, feelings and instincts.

Most people have good intentions when they are giving advice, but remember, they are not you. They have a limited frame of reference from what they are basing their advice on.

They don't see the whole picture of who you really are. They don't know what might be hidden deep within you.

In the hierarchy of influence, make sure your feelings and beliefs are at the top when you are making decisions. Never be afraid to stand up for what you want, even if it is not what others think you should do. You do know what's best for you.

We All Make Mistakes

Another reason why we don't take our own advice is that we are fearful of making a wrong decision. It is much easier for the pain of a wrong decision to be placed on somebody else's advice rather than your own. If our decisions come from us, then there is no one else to blame.

We all make mistakes, and even when you make a mistake, you don't need to dismiss your ability and faith in yourself to know what's best. Given all the information at that particular time and place, you chose what you thought was best for you. The good news is all your bad decisions and mistakes will help you make better choices in the future.

Quiet Your Mind And Listen To Yourself

Asking yourself the right questions is vital to tapping into your innate wisdom. It is also important to be in the right frame of mind when you are asking the questions. Have you ever made a poor decision when you have been tired, overly stressed or inebriated? That decision to "drunk text" your ex at 2 A.M. didn't end up so well, did it?

It is important to be as clear, calm and relaxed as possible when you are contemplating big questions in your life. When your mind is stressed or overstimulated, it can be difficult to receive helpful answers. It might seem like you must not know what to do and decide you should start looking outside yourself for guidance. Maybe you should go see who is at the bus stop.

The truth is you do have the answers; it's just that you need to be in a mental space that will allow you to find them. There are several steps that you can do to put yourself in the right frame of mind before asking yourself questions. The first step is to find a quiet place where you will not be disturbed. It doesn't have to be anywhere fancy; it could just be sitting in your car in a parking lot.

The next step is to take a few deep breaths and center yourself in the moment. Clear your mind of any and all thoughts, especially negative ones. Take a few more deep breaths and feel your body starting to relax. Keep breathing deeply and after a few minutes, there will be no tension in your body. Your mind will now be ready to answer your questions.

Think of what answer you are looking for and form questions that will give you the most direct answers. Make sure you do not phrase the questions negatively. Focus on the questions and continue to breathe deeply. Don't feel like you have to come up with the answers immediately. There is no need to pressure yourself or feel anxiety about the amount of time it will take to come up with answers. If you find your mind wandering, gently bring it back to the question you are asking.

Soon you will notice answers revealing themselves to you. Resist the urge to immediately attack or reject the answers that come to you. Allow yourself the freedom to listen to the answers with an open mind. Look for reasons why they will work rather than reasons why they will fail. You will find solutions to overcome any obstacles and challenges you might think of. It is a wonderful feeling when you realize anything and everything is possible.

The more you practice your ability to look within for answers, the stronger your belief will be that you know best. Soon, you will no longer be swayed by outside influences. You have taken control of your life and are tapping into knowledge only you possess. Congratulations, you are now the smartest person on the planet, at least when it comes to knowing what is best for you. Feel free to introduce yourself as a guru at your next social gathering.

Chapter Summary

- You are the best source of knowledge for all your questions

- Ask yourself positive leading questions instead of negative leading questions

- Trust and believe that you know what is best for you

- Learn to quiet your mind and listen to yourself

Action Plan

Think about how you talk to yourself and what questions you ask yourself. Write down any negative questions you ask yourself.

Example: Why don't people like me?

1. _____

2. _____

3. _____

4. _____

5. _____

Now flip those questions into a positive.

Example: Why do people like me?

1. _____

2. _____

3. _____

4. _____

5. _____

Now ask yourself both sets of questions. Was your mind able to find answers to all of them? Which answers made you feel better? When you catch yourself asking negative leading questions, flip them to a positive and you will feel better and find more helpful answers.

Write down some of your desires that you have been having difficulty in coming up with ways to make it your reality.

Example: How am I going to find a new romantic partner? How can I make more money? How can I be happier at my job?

1. _____

2. _____

3. _____

4. _____

5. _____

Pick one of the above items and find a quiet place where you will not be disturbed. Start breathing deeply and begin to relax. Clear your mind of all negative thoughts and outside influences. Believe that you will find the answers to make your desire a reality. Ask yourself positive leading questions about how you can make your dreams come true. Write down the answers you receive.

1. _____

2. _____

3. _____

4. _____

5. _____

Were you surprised at how many answers you received to each question?

Did you come up with opportunities that you didn't think of in the past?

You can do this exercise for all your dreams and desires. The cool thing about doing the above exercise is that your mind will continue working in the background to come up with more answers for you. You might find new ideas and solutions popping up into your mind even after you have left your quiet space.

Daily Action:

1. Place yourself at the top of the knowledge scale.

2. Believe that you have the knowledge to answer all your questions.

3. Always ask yourself positive leading questions.

4. Practice calming your mind and tapping into your wisdom.

5. Have fun experimenting with different questions to see how efficient your mind is when you ask it the right questions.

"Happiness is not something ready-made. It comes from your own actions."

- Dalai Lama

Chapter 6: The Two Keys To Happiness

One of the cornerstones of living your Big Juicy Life is to be happy. Happiness is the ultimate goal for your life. If someone were to ask me if I could have just one wish, what would it be? It wouldn't be for a million dollars or a fire red Ferrari, or even a supermodel girlfriend. I would just wish to be happy every day.

If I was granted my wish, it wouldn't really matter how much money I had, who I was dating or what kind of car I drove. If I was happy every day, the details of all those areas have already fallen into perfect alignment. There is a big lesson there. The way to find happiness is to concentrate on happiness itself and not on a specific item, person or goal.

Now don't get me wrong, I would have no problem accepting those other three choices, but the truth is they would not guarantee happiness. Many people who are rich, famous and seem to have everything a person could want, are absolutely miserable. How could that possibly be?

We all want to be happy, but it seems like in many cases it's quite elusive. Often there is a sense of lack, a sense of missing something in our lives. We can spend much of our time trying to figure out what the missing piece is. We find ourselves believing that "If I only had (fill in the blank), then I could be happy." And even though many times, we end up getting what we wanted, we are still unhappy and we end up repeating that same cycle.

In this chapter I am going to show you the process to having more joy in your life. This process includes two keys to finding more happiness. They are simple to use and will work for everyone. They are not complicated to understand or to put into your daily life. Once you understand these two principles, you can use them anytime you want to bring more joy into your life.

Before I give you the two keys to happiness, let me share a story about my frustrating journey of trying to find happiness for myself.

Stuck On The Escalator

The truth is I have lived a great life, but another truth would be I constantly struggled to find happiness. On the outside, it looked like my life was great. It didn't look like I was lacking in any area. I was good looking and had plenty of girlfriends. I had a great career. I had money in the bank and expensive cars. I was outgoing and funny, usually the life of the party. It seemed like I had everything I could want, but I still felt unsatisfied.

I figured the reason why I was not able to be happy was because I don't have enough yet. I must still be lacking in several areas. I then filled my life with the pursuit of more. I wanted more money, more recognition, more women, more everything. I believed that if I just had a little more, then I could be happy. Have you ever felt like that?

I was very good at getting more. And when I got more, I would feel happy for the moment, but it would quickly fade away. I then set the bar a little higher, each time believing that if I get it this time, it will finally bring me the happiness I so desperately desired. This pattern kept repeating itself over many years. As time went on, the temporary joy of getting more started to wear off like an overused drug. I began to realize the path to happiness was not about getting more. It was all an illusion.

I took a hard look at my life and saw how much time and energy I had spent on chasing happiness the wrong way. I realized it did not matter how much I got, it was never going to bring me happiness. Let me try to paint you a picture of the painful realization I discovered.

I felt like I was walking up a down escalator, about halfway to the top. At the top of the escalator, I could see my happiness. I could imagine what it would be like and how good it will feel when I get there. I was excited because it did not seem that far away. All I had to do was keep taking steps and I would get there.

I was constantly moving, but I wasn't getting any higher. It seemed like with every step higher I took, the escalator moved me down the same amount. I did not realize this at first and I was convinced that I was still getting closer to my happiness. It did not matter if I walked slowly or fast, I always stayed in the same spot. I was stuck in the middle. I realized I was never going to get to my happiness on that escalator.

That realization of knowing I was never going to get there was heartbreaking. I wondered if it just wasn't my destiny to be a happy person. I tried to return to my old ways of getting more. Even though I knew it was not the way to my happiness, I figured it might make me feel better. It didn't. It was like watching a magic trick after you found out how it is done, the thrill is gone. It is not enjoyable anymore.

After sitting in my sadness for quite some time, I decided that there has to be a way to have happiness that I have been missing. I thought there had to be a formula that I had not discovered. I was determined to find the keys to happiness. I realized that I had to take a look at life differently if I was going to find the principles to happiness.

I studied religion and spirituality looking for the path to happiness. It appeared that in most teachings, happiness is not determined by getting specific things or achieving certain goals. Happiness resided in a more ethereal and emotional state. All that was great, but how does that correlate into the real world? I did not want to become a monk and meditate all day. I needed to find something that was more realistic and readily available.

I began looking all around the world for more clues. I started to watch people and see when they were smiling and laughing. I started taking notes when it looked like people were happy. I began to notice a pattern and boiled it down to two principles.

I began experimenting with them in my own life. I quickly realized that they worked. Using these two keys was quite easy and did not require money or any material thing. You did not even need to shave your head, give away all your money or eat gluten free.

These two keys will work for everyone, no matter who you are and what your personal life journey has been. You can put them into use today. They can bring you more joy whenever you want. It is my pleasure to give you the two keys to finding happiness.

Action And Connection

The two keys to finding happiness are action and connection. These two principles will allow anyone to bring more joy into their life. It is a recipe that can be duplicated over and over again. These two keys also allow for an infinite combination of ways to be happy.

Having more joy in your life requires a paradigm shift in the way you understand happiness. The real path to happiness is not about having a lot, getting more, or being more. It is about being able to experience joy, right here, right now.

Many people are obsessed about planning something in the future that they think will unlock their happiness. It could be when they get that job, when they get that car, or when they meet the person of their dreams, and then they will be happy.

Waiting to be happy at some point in the future is no way to live. The truth is happiness can only be experienced in the present moment, not in the future. The good news is you do not need to wait for anything, you can be happy today, no matter what your life experience currently is.

Once you understand that you can have happiness now, you will stop putting so many demands on yourself to have more and be more. You can begin to relax and by using these two principles, you will find that being happy is easier than ever before. Let's take a look at the first key, Action.

Action

By our physical nature, we are designed to move. Everything about our physical form is built for motion. Not just linear motion or two-dimensional motion, but 3-D dynamic motion, and lots of it. We can run for miles, we can climb high mountains, and we can even do somersaults, spins and twirls. The amount of movement we are capable of is amazing.

We are also blessed with having our five senses. Our senses of taste, touch, smell, hearing and sight allow us to deeply experience the world around us and everything in it. Even by just walking down the street, it can be a sensory explosion of sights, smells and sounds.

Action also takes other forms rather than just physical motion and using our senses. Action also includes our ability to communicate with other people. Our ability to share our thoughts, wisdom and feelings with others is one of the biggest gifts of language.

The truth is there are endless ways that we can take action and there is a good reason for this. It is through action that we are able to have unlimited opportunities to find happiness. It is through action that we are able to interact with people, places and things in our world. It is through these interactions that we will find joy.

Action by itself though is not enough to bring us joy. Many people try to stay busy all the time, hoping it will make them feel happy, but it doesn't work. The reason is because there is another key that is needed to turn the action into happiness. The other piece of the happiness puzzle is connection.

Connection

The other key to finding happiness is connection. It is not enough to just take action, there needs to be an emotion that is experienced during the action. The action needs to generate a good feeling within you. It could be a feeling of love, a sense of awe, or a feeling of giddiness and delight. There is a wide array of good emotions that your actions can make you feel.

The connection part of action is what is missing from so many people's lives. You probably know people who have full business and social calendars. You might think they must be quite happy. The truth is it doesn't matter how busy they are. If they are not making connections, then they are just going through the motions without the emotion. That is like being a zombie. Don't be a member of the undead; you are here to make connections to everything all around you.

One of the best ways to find joy is to connect with other people. There are so many people in this world that can add happiness to your life in so many different ways. One of the easiest ways to connect with people is by talking with them. Unfortunately, many people have lost the art of conversation.

It seems like so many people are too easily distracted and do not give other people their full attention. When was the last time you truly paid attention to what a person was saying at a party? Were you half-heartedly listening to them while silently wondering when the next shrimp platter will be coming out? Most of us have gotten very good at automatically tuning out when we are talking with new people. You are missing out on lots of joy by not being able to be present and active during conversations.

You will be surprised at how much more enjoyable the world becomes when you can have conversations and connect with all the amazing and diverse people all around you. There are so many different things that people can offer you that can make you feel connected. You might meet someone who shares your political views. You might meet someone who makes you laugh. You might meet someone who makes your heart flutter. All these interactions can bring you a sense of joy.

The thing to remember is we do not know what emotion people can offer us until we actually talk to them. Wouldn't it be great if everyone at the party had a sign that advertised what they can offer you? One person could have a sign that says I can make you laugh, another person might have a sign that says they can teach you how to cook, and yet another person might have a sign that says I can make your toes curl. Even though people do not wear those signs, you might be surprised at who you can meet that will change your life if you just start talking to them.

Connections with other people are not just about having conversations with them. You can also feel connected when you have a shared experience with other people. It could be by attending a class or seminar together. It could be by traveling together, or it could be by watching a concert or sporting event.

It amazes me when I watch a football game and look at the people in the stands. You can see the joy on their faces. The reason they are feeling happy is because they are experiencing emotions while having a shared experience with all the people around them. They are joined by thousands of people in the stadium rooting for the same team. They are high-fiving people who they never met before, laughing and getting excited with strangers. It is no wonder why tickets to live sporting events are in high demand.

Connections Are Not Just With People

There are endless opportunities to form connections with everything and everyone around you. Connections don't have to be just with people. Connections can be with places, pets, and things. Many times we focus just on being connected with people. You are missing out on a lot of happiness by not seeing there are so many other ways to connect with the world around you.

Some of the strongest connections can be made with animals. There is something magical that happens inside us when we look at, pet or play with an animal. It seems like our heart fills with love and we revert to being a child again. The joy of connecting with an animal is one of the most beautiful experiences you can have. It is no wonder that our pets play such an important role in our lives.

If you have never allowed yourself the opportunity to make a connection to an animal, I encourage you to find a petting zoo. Petting an animal is one of the most relaxing things you can do. You might feel all your problems melting away and feel good knowing that you share the world with amazing creatures like the one in front of you. You can also ask a friend if you could come over and play with their dog or cat. You will be surprised at how quickly it can bring a smile to your face.

You can also connect to the environment and all the amazing places in our world. It is easy to develop emotions by experiencing nature on a deeper level. If you have ever walked among the redwood trees, it would be hard not to feel a sense of awe. If you have ever stood at the side of the Grand Canyon, it would be hard not to have your heart quicken a little bit and feel excited. Even sitting on a beach and watching the waves crash on the shoreline at sunset can move you to tears.

The good news is you do not have to travel far to find the beauty of nature. There is beauty everywhere, from the fluttering butterfly to the clouds in the sky. I bet there are even areas in your hometown that you have forgotten how beautiful they are. When was the last time you stopped for a moment and allowed a piece of nature to sink in and let it develop an emotion in you?

There many other things you can feel connected to also. You can feel connected to playing or listening to music, watching a movie, reading a book, painting a picture, or seeing works of art. The list is endless. Just remember, the test of whether or not you are connected to something is do you feel an emotion? When you are connected to something, you feel good. You feel happy.

How To Add More Connection In Your Life

The great news is that it is so easy to add more connection into your life. The first step is to purposefully set an intention of trying to make a connection in all your actions. It is amazing how quickly you will find more connections just by setting that as your intention.

The next step is to choose different actions than you have done in the past. When you are talking with people, give them your full attention and be an active participant in the conversation. You will be surprised at how much more enjoyable conversations are when you are not distracted.

Do not be in such a hurry all the time. Take a look everywhere you go and see if you can spot the beauty all around you. Clear your mind and just soak in your environment until it generates an emotion in you. Suddenly you will feel like you have found a hidden world that many people do not see.

Start finding more joy while doing the things you currently do. Even everyday events can bring you joy when you spice them up a little bit. Put on some of your favorite music while making dinner. Dance around the kitchen as you prepare yourself a nice meal. Sing your favorite songs in the shower. Walk outside when you have your morning coffee and listen to the birds sing. These little changes can make it easy to have more fun without even leaving your house.

Take More Action

In order to add more happiness in your life, you need to take more action. It is time to get off the couch, say yes to invitations and start changing things up! Many times, we can get a little isolated in our lives. We get comfortable in the ability to have our food delivered, buy everything online and communicate with friends and family over the internet. You need to start getting out more.

There is something magical that happens when you are out and about in the world. You end up seeing new things, having new experiences and meeting new people. Let me ask you a question, how many new people have you ever met sitting on your couch at home?

Have faith and believe that every time you leave the house, something good will come from it. It is time to stop coming up with excuses when you are invited to go see a movie, meet for coffee or go to lunch. The more you say no, the more you are missing out on new opportunities for love, joy and success. Remember, you do not know what good could come from taking action until you actually take it.

Be Systematically Unsystematic

Not only do you need to take more action to find more happiness, you need to take different action. Many of us tend to be creatures of habit. We do the same things over and over again. We eat at the same restaurants, we go to the same supermarket and we go to the same park. If you want to experience more happiness, then it is time to shake things up.

Let me tell you about a technique that will guarantee your life will not be the "same old same old." This principle will insure you will meet new people, see new things and have new experiences. This magical technique is called systematically unsystematic. That might sound like a Dr. Seuss book, but it is a real thing.

What it means is that you purposefully make sure you do not do things in a consistent way. You constantly change your patterns and routines. I was first taught this technique as a police officer. Let me give you an example of how it works. As a police officer, it would be bad to fall into a routine. It would not take long for the bad guys to know when I did building checks, ran radar or ate lunch, if I did them at the same time every day. This could be dangerous for me and allow the criminals to plan their crime.

By varying the times and places I would go to, the criminals would not be able to anticipate where I would be and when I would show up. It is this element of surprise that can prevent crime from happening. Now let me show you how this element of surprise can work to add more love, joy and success in your life.

When you start changing the routines of your everyday life, you are opening yourself up to many more opportunities to meet new people, see new things and have new experiences. It is through these new interactions that you will have pleasant surprises. Perhaps it will be bumping into an old friend, meeting a new friend, or making a new business connection.

It is easy and fun to change up your daily routines. Let's take a look at a few examples. If you get your coffee at the same place every morning, chances are they know your name. You need to start going places where you need to introduce yourself. Make it a plan that you will go to a different place each week to get your coffee.

If you bring your lunch to work every day, once a week go out for lunch. If you go to the same park with your dog all the time, try a new park. If you take the same drive home from work every day, take a different route from time to time. You might find some stores you like that you did not know were on the way home.

These small changes might not seem like a big deal, but they can be magical. When you change things even slightly in your life, you are automatically rearranging the Universe in untold ways. You can think of it as the "butterfly effect". Just one small change can make all the difference in the world. Because of that one simple change, it allowed you to have a chance encounter to meet someone that will change your life forever.

Be Bold

I hope you are now excited to start changing things up in your life. I have one last piece of advice for you. Be bold!

There are so many times when we hesitate in saying "Hi" or smiling back at someone. There are so many opportunities for new friendships and new experiences that we miss out on by being timid. What are you so afraid of? People don't bite, and even if they do bite, chances are they don't have rabies.

Think about some examples of how a chance encounter brought a new friend, lover, or experience into your life. Maybe you bumped into them at a store or struck up a conversation while you were in the checkout line. What would you have missed out on if you looked the other way or didn't talk to them?

The universe is always giving you opportunities to meet new people. Remember though, nobody is wearing a sign telling you how they can contribute to making your life better; you have to talk to them. So the next time you feel like talking to someone but start to hesitate, take a deep breath, smile and just say "Hi".

Disclaimer: I am not responsible if you do get bitten and end up contracting rabies.

Chapter Summary

- Happiness is the ultimate goal for your life

- Just keeping busy is not enough to be happy

- You can easily find happiness by taking action and making a connection

- Action comes in many forms

- Connections are not just with people. They can be with animals, places and things

- Be systematically unsystematic to give yourself new opportunities to find more love, joy and success

- Be bold and say "Yes" to invitations and opportunities

Action Plan

Write down the ways you currently take action that bring you joy.

Example: I like to take my dog to the park and play fetch.

1. _____

2. _____

3. _____

4. _____

Do you see that it is the combination of action and feeling an emotion that make you feel joy? Would you still feel happy if you still did the action, but did not feel an emotion?

Write down some new ways you can take more action in your life that will give you new opportunities to feel a connection.

Example: I am going to go hiking in nature. I am going to join a book club. I am going to go to an art museum.

1. _____

2. _____

3. _____

4. _____

Be open to trying new activities. You might be surprised at how much joy you have been missing out on by not being adventurous.

Daily Action:

1. Make a conscious effort to include more of the actions that bring you joy.

2. Look for the beauty all around you and let it generate a feeling within you.

3. Say "Yes" instead of "No" to invitations and opportunities.

4. Change your routines. Do something different on a consistent basis.

5. Do not be afraid to start conversations with people.

6. When talking with people, use more than one word answers. Ask questions of the other person to get to know them better and keep the conversation going.

"By changing nothing, nothing changes."

-Tony Robbins

Chapter 7: Embracing Change

Have you ever felt like change sucks? It always seems to come at the worst possible time. Usually it is the last thing you were expecting. Just when you thought everything was going great, you get hit with an unexpected circumstance. Change can definitely shake up your world and not in a good way. It is no wonder that many of us try to resist change. Unfortunately, our resistance usually ends up making the situation even worse.

The truth is everything about your life is designed for change. Although many of us try to prevent it at all costs, we are powerless to stop it. You might try to remain as motionless as possible in an attempt to try and keep everything just the way it is. But even when you are standing still, you are actually whizzing through the universe as the earth is spinning at 10,000 miles per hour. Now where did I put my motion sickness pills?

Every day, things are changing. Our environment and everything around us is different than the day before, however so slightly. Everything inside us is also changing. Every day, our bodies are creating new cells and discarding old ones. I am not just talking about a few cells changing, but millions daily. I just wish my fat cells would leave on a more frequent basis.

The good news is even though life is always changing, that does not mean that life cannot be enjoyable regardless of what changes. Herein lies one of the secrets to being happy.

In this chapter, I will give you the three steps to embrace change. The first step is perhaps the hardest. That step is to accept the fact that everything changes and nothing stays the same forever. The second step is to assess the situation honestly and see what your options are for moving forward. It is important that you focus on what the future can bring rather than get stuck in longing for the past. The third step is to take more control of your life and make decisions instead of waiting for things to happen.

The truth is change is a beautiful thing. It is what allows us to live a Big Juicy Life. Change forces us to take action and make decisions that we never would have taken if the change didn't happen. There is a magical beauty to how change can bring us more love, joy and success that we didn't even know was possible. Here is a story that made me see the beauty of change in my life.

From Police Officer To Star Trek Actor

I have been through many big changes in my life. Most of them were not by my choice. They were made by other people or situations beyond my control. I have always tried to maintain control over everything in my life, but when the shit hits the fan, it seems to happen in a big way.

In 1998, my life fell apart. It seemed like everything I worked so hard to create and hold onto had crumbled. My long term relationship unexpectedly ended, my chances for a promotion at work were zero, and it seemed like everything I was comfortable with was now different. I didn't want things to change in my life, but they did. I could no longer stay in denial about what was happening. My life was at a crossroads.

I was forced to make some hard decisions about where my life was headed. I felt stuck in all areas of my life. I decided to reinvent myself and get a change of scenery. I left my job as a police officer, sold my house, my motorcycle and pretty much everything else I owned. I said goodbye to New Jersey and headed off to Las Vegas.

I figured my life couldn't get any worse at this point, so I wanted to try my luck somewhere new. What better place to get lucky than Las Vegas. It was the place where all your dreams come true; that is if your dreams consisted of losing all your money, becoming an alcoholic and living on the streets. Plus I had heard that Las Vegas was the best place to find yourself...in prison. I was looking to be happier and heard that joy was easy to find there, she was the girl on the street corner with the blond wig. Ok, no more jokes about Las Vegas. The truth is I had gone there on vacation and liked it, plus I had family living there.

After 5 days of driving cross country, I finally arrived at the apartment I had rented sight unseen. I got my keys and opened the door to my new home. I took a look around and began to feel sick to my stomach. I couldn't believe this was where I would now be living. I had left a beautiful house with hardwood floors and a hot tub. I had a sunken living room with a full brick wall fireplace and big bay windows looking out into my large backyard. And now here I was living in a small one-bedroom apartment in Las Vegas, overlooking a dumpster.

I sat on the living room floor and wondered how in the hell did my life end up like this. This isn't what my life is supposed to be. This isn't where I thought I would be in my life. It seemed like I had lost everything. Tears began streaming down my face.

I wondered why all this happened to me. I could not stop replaying the events in my mind of what happened that caused the big changes in my life. I did not deserve what had brought me to this place. It wasn't fair dammit!

I felt like I was all alone in the world. Luckily I had my dog there to give me a pep talk and tell me everything was going to be ok. She kissed the tears off my face and I was determined to move forward with my life.

As time went by, I began meeting new people in my neighborhood. I met a neighbor who said she was a "casting agent" for a modeling agency. She approached me one day and said "You are a good looking guy, did you ever do any modeling?" I immediately wondered if this was to be the beginning of my porn career. Just kidding, she turned out to be a legitimate casting agent.

Even though I had never done any modeling before, she hired me to be in a couple commercials for one of the big casinos on the strip. They dressed me up in expensive clothes and put me with different people in different scenes. It was a lot of fun. It suddenly dawned on me that this could be the beginning of my new career. I had always dreamed of being an actor, so why not go for it.

I applied for the first acting job I saw and was invited to come in for an audition. I didn't know what to expect. I tried to remember anything I could from when I had an acting class in college. Sadly, I didn't remember a damn thing. Why didn't I pay more attention?

During the audition, I had to read several scripts as different characters. I also had to perform some improv comedy. I remember the director put me in a contorted body position and said I just had to go with it. I had always been quick witted and I was able to rattle off a few jokes.

As I left the audition, I thought I did pretty well. I couldn't help but smile and congratulate myself for even having the guts to go for it. I thought even if I did not get the part, it felt good to put myself out there and chase a dream I've had for a long time.

I wondered how long it would be before I heard anything. I didn't have to wait long, later that day I received a call that I had gotten the job. Holy cow I thought, I'm going to be an actor!

The next day I went to the wardrobe department for my costume fitting. As the seamstress was taking my measurements, she told me what accessories I needed to purchase to go with my costume. One of those items was a thong. I thought she was just joking with me and I laughed heartily. She didn't laugh and repeated the statement that I needed a thong. I again laughed and smiled. Then she looked at me quite seriously and said you really do need a thong. These costumes are skintight and you can't have any underwear lines.

The smile disappeared from my face and my mouth got dry. I've always considered myself a little edgy with my colored underwear, but wearing a thong was a whole other animal. I felt a sense of dread come over me and I wondered what the hell did I just get myself into.

Where does one even get a thong for men? I didn't think Victoria's Secret had a men's section. But I figured in Vegas, there had to be a place for men to buy thongs. It turns out there are lots of places in Las Vegas to buy men's thongs, but it was difficult to find ones that were not a cheetah print or had an elephant's trunk attached to the front. Luckily I found some plain colored ones and was now all set.

My new job as a full time actor had begun. I was now a Starfleet Officer in Star Trek: The Experience. It was an interactive Star Trek themed attraction which included live actors at the Las Vegas Hilton. It was an immersive show where people were teleported to The Enterprise. It was an amazing experience for hardcore and casual fans alike. The attention to detail was incredible. They recreated the bridge of the Enterprise to be an exact replica of the one from the television series.

I enjoyed working in such a fun environment and my fellow actors were amazing. I had never been around such a group of eclectic and talented people before. I started to make friends with them outside of work. Who would have thought I would ever have Klingons for friends?

I loved my job as a Starfleet Officer. I would smile everyday as I would zip up my costume. I could not help but laugh at the irony of life. A little more than a year ago, I was a police officer with 14 years of experience, and now, here I was, standing on the bridge of The Enterprise in a spandex jumpsuit, wearing a thong.

Many days it seemed quite surreal to me. Never in a million years could I have foreseen or predicted where I was now at in my life. This was one hell of a change. Talk about a plot twist, I didn't see this in the brochure.

I thought about how much less stressed I was about going to work. Where before I would worry about what danger I might run into as a police officer, now the only thing I worried about was blowing one of my lines. It felt good to not be stressed out at a job. I didn't know a job could be this fun.

I thought of the contrast that the changes in my life had given me. I had an epiphany which made me realize that if my life had not taken the nose dive in New Jersey, I would never be living in Las Vegas having fun as an actor. Even though the events in New Jersey were the hardest times of my life, I could see that because of them, I was presented new opportunities for happiness. I wouldn't want to go through what I went through again, but because of what happened, I was able to make a new life for myself and discover more love, joy and success.

Go With The Flow

In your life, there are many things that are truly beyond your control. It doesn't matter how well you plan, organize, or envision the future. Unforeseen circumstances will happen. Even though they can be very painful, they also serve a bigger purpose. Unexpected change is part of life's magical plan to enhance your experience while you are on this planet.

It can be hard to see the value of unexpected changes while they are causing you so much pain. But when you deny or resist the change, it has a tendency to make you feel even worse. The best thing you can do is to try to relax and stop resisting what is occurring.

It doesn't make sense that when things get out of control, you should lessen your grip on the reins of your life. It seems like it makes more sense to try harder, resist the change and look for ways to make it go back to the way things were. The truth is that when you resist change, you are fighting a force you simply cannot win.

When you are faced with unexpected changes, it is best to go with the flow. Let me illustrate an example of how going with the flow makes your journey easier. Picture yourself standing in the middle of a river. The water is knee high and you can feel the water rushing by your legs. Even though the water is trying to push you in the direction the water is flowing, you are able to resist the force and stand there easily.

Now picture yourself walking against the current of the river. It seems like the current is stronger than when you were standing still. Each time you raise your foot, the current is trying to force you backwards. Your steps forward become harder and harder. If you were to continue to walk against the current, you would quickly grow tired and weak.

Now imagine yourself walking with the current. Feel the difference from when you were walking against it. See how easily your steps are made. It seems like each time you raise your foot, the river is pushing you forward, encouraging you to go in that direction. The current is helping you conserve your energy and allowing you to walk even further than if you were on dry land. You are now in sync with the flow of the water.

The river visualization represents the stream of experiences and situations in your life. It is helpful to move forward with the changes in your life rather than resist them and try to go backwards. Resisting change can drain you emotionally, physically, and spiritually. It is best to use your energy to see which path forward you should take that will make the best outcome from a bad situation.

The Beauty Of Change

When you begin to release your demand that everything stays the same, you open yourself up to see the beauty of change. The beauty is not always recognizable at first. Many times, it seems like the change is terrible and there is no possibility that any good could ever come from it.

Take a look back in your life and see if you can remember some unexpected changes that seemed terrible at the time. Did your view of those incidents change over time? Were there some good things that eventually happened because of those events? Chances are there were some positive aspects that the unexpected change also provided.

What if you could embrace change without immediately knowing what good will come from it? When you decide to begin embracing change, you will feel more optimistic about negative situations you find yourself in. You will believe that even though this doesn't feel good right now, there will be some good that will come from it. It might not be apparent today or even next year, but life has a neat way of forcing you to change that will eventually help you be happier than ever before.

Take Control Of Your Life

It is not always easy to embrace change. There are many reasons why we resist it. One of the biggest reasons is fear. Have you ever been in a bad situation and wanted to change it, but you thought it might get worse if you tried to make it better? The fear of the unknown can be quite stifling. Many people would rather stay in a bad situation than take a risk by going for something better. You are missing out on so much love and joy by living that way.

While it is best to go with the flow, it is also important to direct the flow. When was the last time you took a look at your life to see what is working and what isn't? It's time to embrace your ability to affect your life experience. It's time to take control of your life.

Take a look at your life and see what things you would like to change. Perhaps you would like a new job, a new place to live or a more loving and supportive partner. Don't you deserve all those things? Absolutely you do! What is preventing you from pursuing them?

Many times, we let life gently guide us through our existence. We see signs along the way that offer us a glimpse of a happier and more fulfilled life, but we become complacent. We convince ourselves that things are not so bad and there is no need to change anything.

It is only when something big happens that we are jarred out of our complacency. It could be a fight with your partner, getting turned down for a raise at work, or your car breaking down on the highway. When those events happen, suddenly you see clearly that things are not so good and something needs to change.

The truth is in most cases, the problems did not happen overnight. You probably haven't been happy with your partner for some time, you have been repeatedly unappreciated at work and your car has been steadily getting more unreliable.

Instead of taking action when you first started seeing a problem, you decide to wait and hope things will get better on their own. When the same problems happen again, you finally decide that action must be taken. You take a few small steps, but after a few days, your sense of urgency disappears and you go back to living the same way as before. Does that sound familiar?

What happens though is that the events will keep recurring, usually with more emotional pain. Every time you swear that this time you will do something about it. But just as in the past, you talk yourself out of taking the risks, and don't realize the beauty and power of embracing the change you can make yourself.

Make A Choice While You Still Have The Choice

When you let negative situations repeat themselves, they will eventually build up to a moment where you will be forced to make a change. You are now in a situation where you must make a major decision. Usually it is a decision that could have been made a considerable amount of time ago without as much drama or impact. Usually at those critical moments you will have far fewer options than if you took control when these events first started occurring.

Let's take the example of your car breaking down. Because you ignored the small repairs on your car, they have now materialized into a large mechanical failure. Now you need to decide to buy a new car or spend thousands repairing the car you already have. Either one is an expensive proposition. You wouldn't be in that position if you took action prior to your car breaking down. You could have made the small repairs in the past or sold your car when it was still running well and put the money towards a new car.

It doesn't matter if the situation is a bad relationship, poor health, an unfulfilling job or an unreliable car, the key is to be able to start identifying your desire for change and take action before the situation gets out of control. One of the biggest mistakes is to believe they will miraculously get better on their own – that is rarely the case – it is up to you to embrace change and be bold in knowing that you are in control of your life.

Overcoming Fear

It can be scary to make changes in your life. When we start to analyze possible outcomes for the different choices we can make, we usually think of the worst case scenarios instead of the best case scenarios. Our imagination is a wonderful tool but it can also scare the hell out of us.

Here is an example of when my thoughts made me paralyzed with fear. When I started thinking about quitting my job many years ago, this was my thought progression when I began to imagine what might happen. "What if I quit my job and can't find work right away? I will lose my house, my car and have to live on the street. I will end up doing drugs and I will die alone." All of a sudden, the prospect of quitting my job didn't seem so appealing.

In order to overcome your fear, it is important to focus on the positive possible outcomes rather than any negative ones. That does not mean don't be realistic, but don't become obsessed with how everything could go wrong and end up being worse than where you are now. You also don't have to know how every little detail will fall into place. Have faith in yourself and trust that things will work out for the best.

Chapter Summary

- Everything in life changes

- Change guarantees you will have a more diverse and fulfilled life

- Accept that things change and look for ways to move forward instead of clinging to the past

- Make decisions while you still have the most options

- Do not be afraid to take risks to improve your life

Action Plan

Write down some events in your life that seemed terrible at the time, but some good things ended up happening because of that situation.

Example: I lost my job, but ended up starting my own successful business.

1. _____

2. _____

3. _____

4. _____

5. _____

Can you see that if those "bad" things didn't happen, you would have never experienced the "good" things that also happened? Change pushes you out of your comfort zone and makes you take risks and chances that you would not do otherwise. It is through those new situations that you can find more love, joy, and success

Make a list of things you would like to change, but have been putting off.

Example: I want to get a better job.

1. _____

2. _____

3. _____

4. _____

5. _____

Have you been taking action to make those desires a reality? If not, what are you waiting for? It is a big mistake to think that things will get better on their own, they rarely do. It is best to take action while you still have the most options available. Take action now so you will not be forced into a decision when you have not had enough time to plan and prepare for the change.

Write down some action steps you commit to doing so that you will be moving forward with your desired changes.

Example: I am going to update my resume and begin applying for new jobs

1. _____

2. _____

3. _____

4. _____

5. _____

Now it is time to start doing the action steps you have created. It will be helpful if you make an action steps checklist for each desired change. Commit to completing the action steps of your plan on a consistent basis.

The good news is this will get you closer to your desires and you will not feel stuck by your situation. You are taking control of your life and not leaving life up to chance. Way to go!

Daily Action:

1. Be more accepting when things do not go according to plan.

2. Try to find the humor in unexpected changes. When things do not go according to plan, yell out "Plot Twist" and then think of how you can make the best out of the situation.

3. Believe there will be some good that will come from "bad" changes.

4. Take action when you realize you are not happy with your current situations. Do not wait.

5. Take risks and believe that by making changes you will find more love, joy and success.

"If you can dream it, you can do it."

-Walt Disney

Chapter 8: Becoming Your Own Superhero

Let me ask you a question. How many unfulfilled desires do you have in your life right now? Do you want a new career? Do you want to learn a new activity or skill? Do you want to write a book? What has been stopping you? Do you feel like you are not smart enough, not good enough, or just plain can't for a million reasons?

Instead of concentrating on the reasons why you can't do something, have you ever focused on the reasons why you can? How do you know you can't do something if you have never even tried? Many people give up on their dreams without even trying. That is no way to live! Living a Big Juicy Life means going after all your dreams. It means being bold and courageous in your pursuit of happiness.

Your limits are only determined by what you believe them to be. The truth is your success will be determined by your own mental state of mind and your determination to succeed. I'm here to tell you that you can become great, and not just great, but you can become your own superhero! The sky is the limit for you my friend, but when was the last time you looked up to the sky instead of down at the ground?

In this chapter, I'm going to show you how to challenge your fears. I will help you find proof in your past that will give you the confidence to go for your desires. You will also find inspiration from others who have achieved what you would like to accomplish. And most importantly, I will show you how to believe in yourself like never before. Let me share a story with you that showed me the power of believing in yourself.

The Skinny Policeman

I was 18 years old and my adult life had just begun. I was 6 feet tall and weighed a mere 150 pounds, I was quite thin. In fact, I was so skinny that in high school I was voted most likely to become a street lamp.

I was working part time at a local supermarket while I attended college. I had a great job at the supermarket. My job was to gather up the shopping carts from the parking lot and push them back into the store. Welcome to the real world.

I was taking criminal justice classes and my plan was to become a lawyer. It seemed like my life was on a good path, but I was unhappy. My friends and girlfriend had gone to college out of state and I felt out of place in my local community college. Law school seemed so far away and I began to consider a different career path.

The town where I worked was accepting applications for police officers and I thought police work would be great for me. I knew a little bit about police work from when I was arrested several times as a juvenile. I am kidding, I never got caught. The truth is I had done some "ride-alongs" with the local police department in High School and I enjoyed them. I decided I was going to apply.

Now being so young, I thought it was doubtful that I would actually get hired. My main goal was to take the test so that I would get some experience for future job opportunities. Even though I doubted my chances of actually getting hired, I was determined to give it my best shot and go for it 100 percent.

There were several phases of testing for the position. The first phase of the testing was a written exam. Even though my grades were currently lousy in college, it didn't mean I wasn't smart, it just meant my heart was not in my studies. I was pleasantly surprised when I learned I came in first on the written exam. I then advanced to the physical fitness portion of the testing.

The day I showed up at the gym for the physical fitness testing, I was shocked. The gym was filled with men who seemed to be twice my size. I thought there was no way I was going to be able to beat these guys in physical fitness.

There were several different testing stations set up throughout the gym. We had to see how many sit-ups, pushups and pullups we could do. There was a shot put throwing station and a jump rope station. There was also a timed mile run for the last test of the day.

At my first testing station, I watched in horror as the men in front of me effortlessly heaved their shot puts across the gym floor. It looked like their shot puts were blasted out of a cannon. When it was my turn, I wound up my body, made a loud grunt and launched my shot put into the air. It went only a few feet before falling to the ground with a weak sounding thud. I realized I was in big trouble by trying to compete with these larger men.

As I worked my way around to the other testing stations, I started to notice something interesting. These other guys were big and muscular, but they weren't able to do many pushups, pullups or sit-ups. And most of them couldn't even jump rope without getting all tangled up in it. Suddenly I was feeling more optimistic. I started thinking maybe I had a chance in this after all. I might have been skinny, but I was strong. I began blasting out push-ups, pullups, and sit-ups. I even jumped rope like Muhammad Ali.

A couple weeks later, I found out I came in second in the physical testing and would advance to the next round. Even though I kept going further in the testing phases, there were many people who told me I would never get hired. They said I was too young and too skinny to get the job. I heard it from my friends, I heard it from police officers who were already on the force and I heard it from strangers. I wasn't discouraged though, I thought what do they know – I will show them.

The next testing phase was sitting for an interview with the mayor and town council. I tried to look presentable and got my long hair cut. I didn't own a suit and had to borrow one from a friend. It must have helped out because I passed the interview. Now there was just one testing phase left, the psychological exam.

I thought the psychological testing was fun, I got to draw some pictures with crayons. It had been awhile since I had done that. Later in the day, we did some role playing as if I was a police officer. One of the scenarios was I had caught a burglar with a stolen computer in his arms. The psychiatrist then asked me how I would react. Even though I had seen every "Dirty Harry" movie ever made, I resisted the urge to say "Drop it punk or I will blow your head off!" It must have been the right choice because I passed the psychological exam.

I had passed all the tests and now was waiting to see what would happen next. Even though I had made it through all the testing with flying colors, nobody believed I would actually be hired. Several months went by without hearing anything. Then, in August of 1984, I was offered a position as a police officer. I gladly accepted and just after turning 19 years old, I was the youngest person ever hired to be a police officer by my department.

There were many people in shock that I was hired. There were more than a few haters who said that even though I had gotten hired, there would be no way I was going to make it through the police academy. I found out I would be attending one of the most prestigious police academies in the country, the New Jersey State Police Academy in Sea Girt, New Jersey. It had a reputation for being extremely difficult in every way imaginable.

I was not afraid of the challenge, but I wondered how bad could it really be? I would soon find out as my 12 weeks of hell began. The training was intense to say the least. Not only were there countless hours of the most intensive physical training imaginable, but there was also intensive coursework and psychological training. What I mean by psychological training is being yelled at from the time you get up to the time you go to bed. It reminded me of the time I stayed at my grandmother's house during one summer.

In all areas, I was pushed beyond what I thought myself or anyone else could endure. Not only in a physical sense, doing physical training until you either puked or passed out, but also in a mental sense. I went from a life of no discipline to extreme discipline. I had never experienced anything like it before. There were rules and regulations for everything. You had to have your shoes shined, your clothes folded and your bed made every day. I never knew making your bed everyday was that important.

After experiencing and successfully overcoming the many challenges the police academy threw at me, it changed me forever. I learned to embrace a new set of personal beliefs that would stay with me for a lifetime. I now believed there was nothing I could not do. Of all the things I have done in my life, I am the proudest of graduating from the New Jersey State Police Academy.

When I got back to my town to begin patrol work, I felt confident that I could handle any situation I might come across. I was mentally and physically prepared to handle a drug bust, a bank robbery, or a high-speed chase. That all sounds quite exciting, but the truth is many of my days in the beginning were occupied by protecting the children of the town working as a fill-in crossing guard.

As people began seeing me around town, my skinny physical size did not go unnoticed. There were comments made about how skinny I was. Even my fellow police officers would joke about my size. I remember I was about to go on patrol one day when a coworker stopped me and said I had a thread hanging off my sleeve. He then said "Oh wait, it is just your arm".

Despite the comments and jokes, I was not discouraged. I used my excellent training and my personality to begin getting comfortable being a police officer. As the years went on, my body got bigger and the skinny jokes stopped. I had overcome many obstacles and challenges to get where I was and I was very happy and proud to be a police officer.

Of all the "what-ifs" in my life, I wonder how my life would have been different if I had listened to the naysayers who said I was too young and too skinny to become a police officer. What if I didn't commit to doing my very best at every phase of the testing? What if I gave up on all the demands in the police academy? Perhaps if I had not chased my dream and given it my all, I might still be gathering up shopping carts at my local supermarket.

Success Is A Mindset

It is often your fears and doubts that are the biggest obstacle in pursuing your dreams. You need a strong mindset to overcome those fears and doubts. You need an "I can" attitude rather than an "I can't" attitude. This applies in all aspects of your life, whether it is in relationships, in business, in school, or in anything else. There is no bigger factor that will determine your success other than your mindset.

So how can you overcome your negative beliefs and doubts? When they enter your mind, you can begin to challenge them and look for reasons why they are not only untrue, but completely unfounded. One of the first things you can do is to look back at your past and see how you have already accomplished many great things.

I bet there are many examples in your life when somebody said you couldn't do something and you did it anyway. Perhaps it was learning a sport, learning to play an instrument, or learning to dance. Remember the reasons they gave you why they said you were not going to be successful. Do any of those sound familiar to what you are telling yourself now? They were wrong before and luckily, you did not let that stop you and you succeeded.

When you begin to have doubts, your past successes will give you the confidence that you will succeed. They are uniquely your own. There is no better proof of what you are capable of than reliving your own past accomplishments. Once you see that you have overcome challenges and obstacles in the past, how could you not believe you could do it again? Remember this phrase when you need a little boost in your self-confidence. "If you did it once, you can do it again, if you can do it again, then you can do it all the time." Now go get'em tiger!

What Can Happen For One, Can Happen For All

When you are having difficulty believing that things are possible, you can look to the external world for inspiration. There are examples all around us of people who have overcome many obstacles and still achieved greatness. In every arena and in every way imaginable, someone has overcome doubts, fears and challenges similar to what you are experiencing.

You can easily find stories about people who were told they were too dumb to start a business, too old to play competitive sports, or too young to make a difference in the world. Some of the most famous people have wonderful stories about overcoming rejection, failure and naysayers.

Here are just a few examples of inspiring true stories. Stephen King, the famous writer, had his first novel rejected 30 times. Colonel Sanders, founder of Kentucky Fried Chicken, started his business at age 64. Michael Jordan, the famous basketball player, was cut from his high school basketball team because his coach said he wasn't good enough.

When you read about their journeys and how they achieved their desires, you need to realize that just like them, you can also be successful. We are all different people on this planet, but many times we feel like so many others are better than us. When we look at others successes, we might believe that we would never be able to do the same thing. Why wouldn't you be able to?

You are no different than any successful person. Remember this statement when you are thinking you are not capable of achieving greatness like other people. "What can happen for one, can happen for all." If it is possible for someone else to do it, then it is possible for you to do it. You just need to tap into an "I can" mindset and do not let rejections or failures deter you from being successful.

Here is an inspirational story about the famous inventor Thomas Edison. It has been said that when Thomas Edison was trying to invent a filament that would be suitable for a lightbulb, he tried 10,000 different ways to make the filament before he found one that would work. After he was finally successful, he was asked about all his previous failures. He reportedly gave this famous quote, "I have not failed. I just found 10,000 ways that won't work." Thomas Edison never gave up and neither should you. Be like Thomas Edison.

It is a curious thing that happens when we see other people accomplishing great feats. As other people have shattered previously held beliefs, their impact changes the beliefs of everyone around them. Many times, successful people have shown us the way to our own greatness. Look to them as guides to help you break through your limiting mindsets. Let me give you an example.

I love the story of the 4-minute mile. For hundreds of years, nobody was able to run a mile in four minutes or less. In 1954, an Englishman named Roger Bannister was the first person to break the 4-minute mile. It was an amazing feat, but what was perhaps even more amazing was the fact that just 2 months later, 2 more people broke the 4-minute mile barrier. This only happened because their old beliefs were shattered and now they believed it was possible. Once they changed their beliefs, they were able to do it too.

When we witness other people accomplishing great things, it shows us that it can be done. When you believe something is possible, then you just have to believe that you can do it. The truth is not only is it possible for you to duplicate what someone else has done, you can also improve on it or do it better. This mindset is what allows our society and civilization to grow and expand exponentially. We are continually breaking old records and shattering any barriers to man's unlimited potential.

Believe! Believe! Believe!

The founder of Ford Motor Company, Henry Ford, is quoted as saying "Whether you think you can or you think you can't, you are right." It is all up to you as to what you will believe about your capabilities. If you have a success mindset, you are unstoppable.

There might be 100 reasons why you cannot do something, but you only need to find one reason why you can. You can be your own worst enemy or your own biggest cheerleader, the choice is yours. Either way, it is always up to you whether or not you will be successful. It does not matter who says you cannot do it, it does not matter what reasons they give you. Your success is not determined on whether or not other people think you can, it all depends on whether you think YOU CAN. Your true potential comes from the inside and not the outside.

When you believe in yourself, you're tapping into a power that will never go away. When you hold onto that power, you cannot be diminished or minimized. You are an unstoppable force to achieve all you desire. You will be unaffected by the naysayers and all the other reasons why it can't be done.

You have been given one of the most powerful gifts to determine what your life experience will be. That gift is the freedom of thought. Other people might give you their opinion and advice but it is impossible for other people to make you change your thinking. You are always the master of your own thoughts. Choose thoughts that energize and motivate you to reach your true potential.

Chapter Summary

- You can achieve whatever you desire

- You need to believe in yourself that you can do it

- If you were successful before, you can be successful again

- Do not listen to the naysayers and haters

- Find inspiration from others' successes

- If someone else has done something, there is no reason why you can't do it too

- Never give up

Action Plan

List some accomplishments from your past that you thought you would never be able to do. Next to them, write the reasons why you doubted yourself.

Example: I graduated from High School. I felt I wasn't smart enough and lacked the dedication.

1. _____

_____

2. _____

_____

3. _____

_____

4. _____

_____

5. _____

_____

Do you see that you overcame your fears and doubts several times already in your life? The truth is you can accomplish anything you set your mind to. If you have been successful in the past, then you can be successful now. Tap into your past successes for inspiration and proof that you are capable of making your desires a reality.

If there was no doubt in your mind that you could accomplish anything you desired, what would you like to do? List your desires below.

Example: Go back to college and get an advanced degree

1. _____

2. _____

3. _____

4. _____

Now that you have remembered your past successes and have identified what your current desires are, it is time to start taking action to make them a reality. The proof that you can be successful is right in front of you. So forget the reasons why you can't do it and start taking action to make your new desires a reality.

List 3 things that you commit to doing this week that will move you forward in achieving one of your above desires.

1. _____

2. _____

3. _____

Now repeat this process every week and soon your desires will become accomplishments! Congratulations!

Daily Action:

1. Always think positively about yourself.

2. Believe that you can do anything.

3. Take the words "I can't" out of your vocabulary.

4. Look for proof of how successful you are in your daily life.

5. Don't get wrapped up in other people's negativity. Stay positive.

6. Never give up!

"All you need is love. But a little chocolate now and then doesn't hurt."
- Charles Schulz

Chapter 9: Having A Juicy Relationship

I know what you're thinking. How can you have a Big Juicy Life without a loving and fulfilling relationship? The answer is you can't. There is no higher expression of joy and happiness than being in love with someone. Being in love makes you sing in the shower, dance in the rain, and not yell at the dog when he pees on the carpet.

We are not meant to be alone in this world, but why are relationships so damn hard? You would think they would be easier because we all want to be in a loving romantic relationship. If we all want the same thing, then why do we experience so many problems?

For many people, it seems like the same problems happen over and over again in their relationships. When we look at why they don't work out, it is easy for us to identify problems with our partners and to clearly see their faults. It is obvious to us that it is the other person that made the relationship so difficult. Now let me ask you a question. Have you ever taken a good look at what your role has been in your failed relationships?

When you get a clear look at what your role is in your failed relationships, it can open the door to breaking the cycle of bad relationships. You will have a better understanding of what goes wrong repeatedly and why. Once you understand these dynamics, you will have a new set of tools to help you have that big juicy relationship you have always dreamed of. You know the one, the one where your partner doesn't care that you hog the covers, eat potato chips in bed and make baby talk when speaking to your dog.

In this chapter, I'm going to show you how to identify negative patterns in your relationships. You will learn how to get to the root of what is really preventing you from having better relationships. I'm going to show you how to release many of your expectations that can make it hard for you to find the love of your life.

I'll show you how to be clear with your words and feelings so there is no miscommunication with a loved one. I'm also going to share with you the best way to determine if you are in a healthy relationship.

Before we get started, you might be wondering where I got all this great relationship advice. You might think I must be highly skilled in the art of having a happy relationship. I would like to tell you that I married my high school sweetheart and have been living happily ever after, but the truth is I have been a failure at making relationships work.

They say that those who can't do something are usually the best ones to teach it. If that is true, then I am the most qualified ever to talk about relationships. I have ruined, sabotaged and made mistakes in more relationships than anyone I know. I've always been a caring and loving person, but I really blew it when it came time to make my relationships work.

I never felt like I was demanding or overbearing in relationships; I just wanted respect, understanding and passion. But it seemed like no matter who I dated, I ended up feeling disrespected, unappreciated and unloved. My insecurities would get activated and I would end up acting like a big jerk.

When issues would arise with my girlfriends, it seemed like they didn't understand where I was coming from. It irritated me they could not see what I saw and I felt that they "Didn't get it". It seemed as if I was stuck repeating the same patterns in all my relationships.

I had an epiphany several years ago that changed my life. I realized that there were so many things that "I didn't get" instead of the other way around. Let me share a story with you of what happened that finally opened my eyes.

Another Failed Relationship

Several years ago, I had rekindled a romance with an ex-girlfriend. We had dated off and on for about 6 years but it always seemed like our timing was off. This time I thought things were going to be different. I felt we were both finally in a place to make things work this time.

We started seeing each other right before Valentine's Day and I asked her how she would like to celebrate. She said she really wanted to go to this fancy steakhouse for dinner. Here is a tip for you, if anyone ever says a restaurant is fancy, it is just a nice way of letting you know that dinner will cost more than your car payment. I was not dissuaded though, I wanted to make her feel special so I decided to splurge on dinner and not take her to the Olive Garden with my 20 percent off coupon.

I was able to get a reservation for 6 pm and we were all set. We decided she would come to my house at 5 and we would go to the restaurant. Now don't any of you send me nasty emails, I did offer to pick her up, but she wanted to meet me at my house.

When Valentine's Day arrived, I was fully prepared for our romantic and special evening. I groomed myself as if I was stepping out of a GQ magazine. I bought a new shirt, got my hair cut and I even went out and bought new cologne. My bottle of Obsession was almost empty anyway.

I began feeling more and more excited as the clock ticked closer to 5 pm. I couldn't wait to begin the best Valentine's Day of my life. I knew this was going to be a night to remember.

As the clock struck 5:00 PM, I started standing by the front door. I knew my girlfriend would be arriving any second and I wanted to greet her with a big hug and a wet kiss. I felt like this must be what my dog feels like when I leave the house and she sits by the door until I return.

As 5:15 PM came and went, my girlfriend had not yet arrived. I started feeling anxiety creep into my body. I didn't like it when she was late, but there was no way I was going to get mad at her for being 15 minutes late. This was Valentine's Day after all.

5:20 PM came and went. My girlfriend was still nowhere to be found. I wondered where she was. I hoped that she hadn't gotten in an accident. I checked my phone to make sure I did not miss her call or text. I thought of calling her, but I did not want her to feel bad about being late. I knew she did not like it when I called and checked to see where she was.

At 5:25 PM, my girlfriend had still not arrived and I received no calls or texts from her. My uneasiness was now slipping into anger. Why hasn't she called or texted me to let me know she is running late? She knows I get upset by that.

Plus, it was getting close to the time where we would be late for our reservation if she did not get here soon. I tried to relax and went and put on more cologne.

At 5:30 PM, a shift occurred in my mind. I went from trying to make excuses for her lateness to reasons why I don't deserve to be treated like this. I went out of my way to make her desire to go to this nice restaurant a reality. I was going to drop several hundred dollars on a nice dinner and she couldn't even be on time? How dare she disrespect me like this. I charged into the bathroom and tried to wash off the cologne I had just put on; she doesn't deserve it!

As 5:35 PM came and went, it seemed like as each minute passed, I became exponentially angrier. I felt like I was turning into The Incredible Hulk. I wanted to start smashing things around my house, but then I realized it only feels good when you can break stuff and not be the one who also has to clean it up later.

At 5:40 PM, I had crossed the threshold of still thinking I could go to dinner and forget about her being late. We were not going to be able to make our reservation on time now. All my plans were being ruined. Why is she doing this to me? Barring some reason other than her fighting off Godzilla on the way to my house, there wasn't going to be a reasonable explanation of why she was this late.

At this point, I was almost hoping she didn't show up at all. I knew there was no way I was going to be able to act like it was ok that she was so late. I knew myself well and we had been in this situation before. I couldn't believe it was happening all over again. I thought things were going to be different this time.

At 5:41 PM, my doorbell rang. I opened the door and there she was, 41 minutes late. We both looked at each other and neither of us said a word. I did a quick visual check to see if she looked like she had been in a car wreck, a gang war or a knife fight. She looked like she was fully intact. Not only was she intact, but she looked stunning.

She stood there in a tight red dress, wearing shiny red lipstick and black high heels. She looked amazing. She looked like she could bring Superman to his knees with just a glance. As she walked in the door, she handed me a bottle of chocolate flavored wine without saying a word.

I was hoping that her beauty would shock me out of the anger I was feeling. I tried to make excuses for her in my mind. It was obvious that she put significant time in preparing for the evening. Maybe she just took a long time trying to look pretty for me. As much as that might have been true, it still didn't explain why she did not contact me to let me know she was running late.

I didn't want to jump down her throat and be accusatory as soon as she walked in the door, so I bit my tongue and tried to put a happy face on. Unfortunately, my happy face probably resembled a five-year-old biting into a lemon. It was not the least bit convincing and she knew I was upset. She said, "You are mad, aren't you?" I knew this was going to be the turning point of the evening.

I knew if I said yes, that we would be breaking up this evening and going our separate ways. I knew that if I wanted to continue dating this girl, I had better get my shit together and calm down. I knew if I said anything other than it's OK, don't worry about it, I would be spending the night alone.

I played out the different scenarios in my mind of what could happen next. I tried to think of ways to turn this horrible situation into a positive one. As much as I wanted to let it go and say everything was ok, I couldn't. I wasn't able to overcome my feeling of being disrespected, unappreciated and unloved.

I told her I was very upset with her. "I went out of my way to make reservations at an expensive restaurant for you and this is what you do to me? There is no way we can make our reservation now, why didn't you call me or text me that you were running late? Why couldn't you just be on time?"

Her body tensed up and I could see her thighs flex underneath her dress. She took a deep breath and coldly said she had lost track of time. She was not soft or apologetic. She seemed to be more upset with me that I was upset with her. I told her that we have now missed our reservation and I no longer wanted to go out to dinner. She said that she knew I was going to be mad and that is why she didn't contact me. That sounded like flawed logic to me.

After a few more sentences, the inevitable happened. The words came out of both our mouths, "Let's break up". Within just minutes of arriving, she was walking back out the door. This was not how I anticipated my Valentine's Day going. I didn't see this in the brochure.

What was supposed to be a magical evening had now turned into The Valentine's Day Nightmare. I tried to figure out what the hell just happened. It wasn't my fault that the night turned out terrible. I had done everything I was supposed to do. I got the reservation, I was ready at 5 pm, and I even smelled good.

It was her fault that things didn't go according to plan. She was late, and not just a few minutes late, she was 41 minutes late to be exact. What kind of person does that? How could she be so disrespectful, unappreciative and selfish? I didn't deserve it.

I spent the rest of the evening on my couch drinking the chocolate flavored wine she left behind. I sat there wondering why I keep dating the wrong women. I started to remember my many breakups in the past when I felt disrespected or unappreciated. I realized many of them happened on holidays. I remembered breaking up with girlfriends on New Year's Eve, Thanksgiving, and even once on Christmas Day. I wondered why holidays were so treacherous to my relationships. After I finished the bottle of wine, I decided to swear off all holidays in the future and then passed out on the couch.

A few days later, I called my new ex-girlfriend on the phone. I wanted to see if she had thought differently about the situation since some time had passed. I thought she might have realized she was wrong and would apologize for what happened. During our conversation though, it was clear that she did not feel any different about the situation and definitely was not apologetic. We went back and forth about what happened and then she said something to me that would change my life forever.

She said "You know Mike, you make a big deal about a lot of stuff. I don't think you want to be happy." Now typically I would have immediately tried to defend myself. I would have given her reasons why I was justified in my actions, but this time for some strange reason, I didn't. I let her finish what she wanted to say and I wished her the best. We hung up the phone and I knew she wasn't the right one for me, but was she right about me? Do I make a big deal about a lot of stuff?

I've always tried to be very honest and introspective with myself. I've always been the type to try to find answers and never deny my issues. I thought I had learned from all my relationship mistakes in the past. I wondered if there was still something I was missing. I began reflecting on my past relationships and suddenly I started seeing a pattern, it was something that I had never noticed before.

As I relived old relationships in my mind, I saw there were many things that I did make a big deal about. I remembered many situations that ended poorly because I felt disrespected and became upset. I began to look deeper at these patterns and my reactions to certain triggers. All of a sudden I could see clearly what a bigger role I had in my relationships not working out.

I started to see the pattern of me being overly sensitive to many perceived slights. I would have strong reactions to something my partner did that made me feel disrespected. I always thought I was justified in my actions because I was not wrong, they were. I began to look at the reality of the situations and see if I could look at them differently than I had in the past. I began to see the ugliness of my reactions to many situations.

As I began replaying old scenarios with ex-girlfriends, I became sick to my stomach. For the first time, I saw clearly how I had overreacted to issues and problems that were minor in nature. I relived past fights, arguments and breakups that were triggered by seemingly small things. Why did I make such a big deal out of those minor issues?

The more I sat with my past relationships, the more I could see I was choosing to be right over my desire to be happy. I started to see there were other ways, better ways, I could have responded to situations. I was overcome with sadness as I realized I had missed out on having a wonderful relationship with so many of the amazing women in my life.

I realized what a fool I had been. I had so many opportunities to get it right with someone and I blew it each and every time. My ex-girlfriends had all moved on with their lives and found the life of their dreams, a life that could have included me at one point in the past. It was heartbreaking. I could also see for the first time how I hurt so many people who truly cared about me. They did not deserve the pain I caused them. I wanted to contact them and tell them I was sorry.

I thought it was best that I keep my apologies to myself though. I am sure they could care less about my big epiphany that I was such a jerk to them. I think they already knew that. I did decide however that sometime in the future I would develop a 12 step program for people who are recovering relationship assholes and make that step the most important one.

I realized that I needed to make some big changes in myself if I was ever going to be able to have a healthy and loving relationship. It wasn't going to matter who I had in my life, I would repeat my pattern of overreacting and make the relationship harder than it needed to be. I needed to get to the bottom of why I was so sensitive and overreacted to certain triggers.

Patterns Of Pain

When we overreact and respond harshly to our partner over small things – there is something deeper going on – there is more to it than what it appears to be at face value. Unless we get to the root of where our strong reactions come from, we will continually repeat the pattern of overreacting. It will be difficult for you to change your behavior until you can begin identifying your patterns of pain.

Looking for negative patterns in your relationships is not about blaming others or even blaming yourself. It is about identifying reoccurring events where you felt hurt and you responded strongly. Many times, your reaction might have caught your partner off guard. They might have asked you why you were getting so upset over such a small thing. That probably did not make you feel any better and just made you more mad, I know it did for me.

The first step to identify your patterns of pain is to start looking at the things that you react most strongly to. Before we go any further, I am not talking about situations where you are abused, have been cheated on or anything like that. There is no excuse for those actions and you are justified in reacting to those as you see fit. I am talking about situations when little events snowballed into a big misunderstanding, a big fight, or even a breakup.

When you start identifying your sensitivities, don't judge yourself or be hard on yourself. We all have different sensitivities to different things. Because of this, our sensitivities make us more prone to feeling pain than other people without those same sensitivities. It is no wonder your partners could not understand why you were getting so upset, they couldn't feel your pain.

Finding The Source Of The Pain

Once you have identified patterns in your relationships of overreacting, it is time to start tracing the pain back to the root. Let me use myself as an example of what I uncovered. There are three things that I am most sensitive to. The first one is when my partner is late. The second sensitivity of mine is when my partner does not listen to what I am saying in our conversation. The third sensitivity is when my partner does not value my wisdom.

Once I identified what my particular sensitivities were, I started to dig deeper and look for what was actually causing my pain. I started to peel back the layers of my justifications for my reactions. I stopped trying to find answers why I was right in getting mad, and started looking at the situation in a different way.

I analyzed why I got mad when my partner was late. I had to look past the rationalization that everybody should be on time. I had to stop my feeling of being right and believing there was nothing wrong with expecting my partner to be on time. If I held onto that like I normally did, the fights in my relationships would keep repeating because I was choosing to be right over being happy. I had to go deeper.

I began asking myself introspective questions. If my partner is late, what does that say about the value of my time? I thought that if the person who cares the most about me doesn't value my time, that must mean my time is not important. If my time is not important, then I am not important. If I am not important, that must mean I am not worthy. If I am not worthy, that must mean I am unlovable.

Suddenly I realized why I would react so strongly to when my partner is late. It was because I was interpreting the situation into the belief that I was unlovable. It is no wonder that I lashed out, it was very painful. Now I could also see how my partners could not understand what a big deal it was to me. They had no idea that by them being late, it had triggered such a deep and powerful insecurity in me.

I started to look at my other sensitivities to see what was at the root. I took a look at why I got upset when my partner doesn't listen to me. If my partner does not listen to me, what does that say about the value of my words? It must mean that my knowledge, thoughts, and opinions have no value. If my knowledge, thoughts, and opinions have no value, that must mean I am not worthy to have someone listen to me. If I am not worthy to have someone listen to me, that must mean I am not enough.

It became clear where my anger and bitterness was coming from when certain events triggered me. It came from my low self-worth and low self-esteem. I was not reacting to the face value actions of my partner; I was reacting to the perceived feeling that I was unworthy and unlovable. It was no wonder why I responded so quickly and vehemently.

When I saw how my overreactions were traced down to how I interpreted those events, I could clearly see where all the emotion was coming from. These negative feelings and beliefs were the roots of why I had issues in so many relationships. I realized I would never have a healthy relationship with anyone unless I addressed my low self-esteem and low self-worth. I had to change my beliefs.

You Can Change Your Beliefs And Perceptions

Do not be upset by what you might have uncovered that has been the true source of your overreactions. Take heart in knowing that you can change the way you feel about yourself. You can change your negative and limiting beliefs into more positive ones. Once you do that, you will no longer get mired down in trying to prove you are right to your partner of why you are justified in your reactions. You will no longer be as harsh and unforgiving of them. You will be able to let things go much easier than ever before. You will suddenly see that your partner is not trying to hurt you on purpose and you will see that they truly do care about you.

There are several ways you can change your beliefs about yourself. The best way is to challenge your negative beliefs by asking yourself to find reasons why they are not true. You can ask yourself to find reasons why your time is valuable, why you are lovable, and why your partner really does care about you. You will easily find many reasons to contradict your negative beliefs. Once you shine light onto your darkest beliefs, you will find that they quickly disappear.

Once you begin to dissolve your negative beliefs, you will be able to start reacting to situations differently than you have in the past. You will be able to realize that you are being triggered and then stop and see what is really going on. You might see if your reaction is appropriate to the situation or if there are negative beliefs that are still there.

Do not be hard on yourself if you are not able to change your negative beliefs as quickly as you like. Be gentle with yourself and believe you will get there. It might take some time to totally get rid of them – but do not give up – you can do it. If you feel comfortable with your partner, you might want to discuss with them what you have realized about your strong reactions to certain triggers. You can ask them to be supportive of you if you occasionally overreact.

Even though we have all dated some frogs, the common denominator in all your bad relationships is you. Once you are able to feel better about yourself and be more loving towards yourself, you will be amazed at how much better your relationships will be. Suddenly, the issues that kept coming up in the past will disappear without any effort. It will seem like you are picking better partners and you are being treated better than ever before.

Have Few Expectations

Have you ever been frustrated in trying to find the right partner? Do all your dates seem to come from the online dating site SingleFrogs.com? Do you ever wonder where the "right one" is hiding? The truth is you could be having trouble finding the right partner because you have too many expectations of who they must be.

Expectations can come in many forms. You might expect your partner to make a six figure income. You might expect your partner to be the best looking person in the room, or perhaps you expect your partner to be a mind reader. The list of expectations can be endless. What are some of your expectations?

Finding the right partner is not an exact science. Many times we think that if we can just find the person who meets all our expectations, then we will have found our perfect partner and live happily ever after. I do not mean to burst your bubble, but love does not work that way. Cupid has a weird sense of humor about matching up people that will be the happiest together. Have you heard stories from your friends or family when they tell you that the person who turned out to be the right one was the farthest from who they thought they would be?

When you are strict in only considering people that meet your expectations, you are missing out on so many other possible "right ones". I am not saying open up the floodgates and go out with anyone who asks, but realize the fewer expectations you have, the more opportunities you will have to find the love of your life.

When you begin to be less strict about whom your partner must be, your dating pool will be much larger. For example, instead of expecting your partner to make 6 figures, your new expectation might be your partner must have a steady job and a car that is not more than 10 years old. A lot more people will fit into the latter category than the former.

The great thing about romantic relationships is that oftentimes you discover that your perfect partner is someone you least expected. Love is a mysterious and wonderful thing and it does not work in logical ways. It helps to not approach love in such a formulaic way. When you have an open mind and open heart, you might be surprised at who that special person is who takes your breath away.

What Is A Healthy Relationship

Many times we get confused as to whether or not we are in a healthy relationship. There are many different criteria we can use to make an assessment. Usually the most common criteria people use is love. The most typical way we try to gauge our relationship is by asking ourselves if we love our partner and do they love us?

Many people think that love is all you need to be happy in a relationship. Unfortunately, that is not the case. It is possible for a couple to love each other and yet both people are absolutely miserable. That does not sound like it makes any sense, but it is true.

When determining if you are in a healthy relationship, the most important factor is not how much you love your partner or how much they love you. It does not matter how good looking your partner is, how much money they have, or how good they are in the kitchen. The best way to determine if you are in a healthy relationship is to ask yourself this one question:

How do I feel about myself when I am with my partner?

This one simple question will give you more insight into the health and happiness of your relationship than any other criteria you might choose. There is nothing more important than the way you feel about yourself when you are with your partner.

When you feel good about yourself in your relationship, you feel comfortable in your own skin. You are happy being who you are and you feel accepted by your partner. You can let all the facets of your personality shine through. You can be goofy, playful or serious whenever you want to. You are free to express yourself in all ways; verbally, emotionally, spiritually, and sexually.

In a healthy relationship, you feel respected and admired. You know you are valued as a person, as well as a lover. You are secure in knowing that your partner loves you and would not do anything to jeopardize losing you. You do not obsess or worry about your partner's feelings and intentions.

If you find yourself not feeling good about yourself in your relationship, it is time to identify the reasons why. Make sure that the reason is not your innate low self-esteem or low self-worth. Once you are sure that it is not because of any inner self esteem issues, ask yourself what is your partner doing that is contributing to your feeling of not feeling good about yourself. Are you unable to just be yourself? Do you feel unappreciated and disrespected? Do you feel like you are walking on eggshells? Do you feel like no matter what you do, it is never enough? Is your partner just not seeing how great you really are?

When you have identified where your negative feelings are coming from, you can decide whether you want to try and make the relationship work or move on. The good news is you now see clearly where your relationship is making you feel unfulfilled. Remember, you are very special and wonderful and someone will love you just the way you are.

Love is the most magical experience on this earth. There is nothing better than to experience love on its many levels. It is easier to find a good relationship when you know what it should feel like. You should feel good about yourself when you are with your partner. Remember, it doesn't matter how much the other person loves you or how much you love them, the most important aspect is how you feel about yourself when you are with that person.

Good Communication Is The Key

Good communication is the foundation of a good relationship. Many times we are not direct in expressing our feelings, desires and concerns. We tend to drop innuendos, hints and suggestions instead of just saying what is really on our mind. Nobody is a mind reader and it is no fun trying to solve the puzzle like on a game show. I'll take "Why are you mad for $500". There is a much better way of communicating.

It is important to be clear and concise when expressing what is on your mind. There is no need to talk about generalities or beat around the bush. If you are upset about something your partner did, don't just say I am not happy with you. Be specific in what has hurt you.

If you are not clear about what is wrong, it can be very frustrating to your partner. Poor communication can quickly snowball out of control. What might have started out as a small issue can grow into a major argument. Always come from a place of love when discussing problems with your partner, but be bold in telling them how you really feel.

Good communication is not only important in times of trouble, it can also make your relationship more fun and exciting. One of the benefits about having great communication is that you become comfortable in asking for what you want. You can explore and grow your relationship like never before.

Being able to ask for what you want from your partner is like finding the magic genie lamp. You will be surprised at all the things you can have, you just have to ask for them. You can ask for anything and everything you desire. You can ask to go to that new restaurant that just opened downtown, you can ask for help with the dishes, or you can ask to try that new position you saw in that Kama Sutra book.

The good news is that when you are comfortable in asking for what you want, your partner will also become bolder in expressing their desires. Soon, you will both be making all of each other's dreams and desires come true. It is all made possible by having good communication.

Chapter Summary

- It is important to identify the negative patterns in your relationships

- See what negative self-belief are the root cause of your strong reactions to certain triggers

- Change your negative self-beliefs into positive ones

- Believe that you are lovable, wonderful and worthy

- Do not limit your possibilities of finding the right partner by having too many expectations

- It is not how much your partner loves you or how much you love them that is most important, it is how you feel about yourself when you are with your partner that is the best gauge of a healthy relationship

- Communicate openly, honestly, and directly with your partner

Action Plan

List some negative feelings that are a pattern in your relationships.

Example: I often feel disrespected and unappreciated.

1. _____

2. _____

3. _____

4. _____

5. _____

What situations trigger those negative feelings?

Example: When my partner is late.

1. _____

2. _____

3. _____

4. _____

5. _____

Now that you have identified your patterns of pain and the associated triggers, it is now time to find out what is the root cause of your negative feelings.

Take a look at your triggers and see if you can trace them back to the underlying negative self-belief you have.

Example: If my partner is late, that must mean my time is not valuable. I am unworthy.

1. _____

_____

2. _____

_____

3. _____

_____

4. _____

_____

Once you have identified your negative self-beliefs, you can change them. Begin to challenge your negative self-beliefs by asking yourself why they are not true. You will find many reasons why you are lovable, worthy, and desirable. Focus on seeing yourself positively instead of negatively. Soon you will feel a shift in the way you think about yourself. This will allow you to be happier, be more open, and be less reactive in relationships.

Another way you can help yourself be less reactive in relationships is to look at your triggers in a different way. Write down statements that change the way you perceive the meaning behind your triggers.

Example: If my partner is late, it doesn't mean that they don't love me. It just means my partner loses track of time often.

1. _____

_____

2. _____

_____

3. _____

_____

4. _____

_____

By looking at your triggers in a different way, you will not respond to them in an explosive and reactive manner. You still might be upset with what the situation is, but you will not overreact. It will be easier to address the triggers in a more constructive way.

Take a look at your expectations of who your partner must be. See if you can broaden them to allow for more opportunities to find the love of your life. List some of your new, more lenient expectations.

1. _____

2. _____

3. _____

4. _____

5. _____

Now you can be more flexible in considering possible partners. It will make your dating pool much larger. Love works in mysterious ways. You might be surprised to see who your perfect partner turns out to be.

Daily Action:

1. Believe that you are a lovable, wonderful and worthy person that deserves to have a great relationship.

2. Be honest and open with your partner. Say what is on your mind and ask for what you want.

3. Do not put a lot of expectations on yourself or your partner. Allow each other to just be who they are.

4. Concentrate on what your partner does right rather than what they do wrong. Remember, nobody is perfect.

5. Have fun with each other. Be silly and playful. Laugh with each other.

6. Be affectionate. Hold hands, kiss, and squeeze their butt in public.

"Ask for what you want and be prepared to get it."
- **Maya Angelou**

Chapter 10: The Power Of Asking

Have you ever been frustrated with not having what you want? Have you ever looked around and it seemed like everyone else was getting what they wanted, so why not you? Did you ever wonder what they are doing that you are not? Do you want to know what the secret is to getting more of what you want?

Have you ever dreamed of walking on a beach and discovering a magical lantern? You rub its well-worn metal and a genie appears. The thankful genie declares he will grant you three wishes. Gleefully you ponder your biggest desires and then ask for what you want. The genie closes his eyes and POOF, your desires have manifested.

The story of the magic lantern has been around for centuries. It is an amazing tale, but there is a very important lesson that is often overlooked. When the genie offers you your wishes, you must put your desires into words. Even as powerful as the genie is, he is not a mind reader.

In order to get what you want from the genie, you have to ask for it. You have to formulate into words what your desires are so the genie knows what to give you. The more specific you are in your requests, the more accurately they will fulfill your desire. Could this be the real point of the story? Yes, it is!

The secret to getting what you want is simple; you have to ask for it. Harnessing the power of asking for what you want can change your life immediately. You can have more of anything and everything you desire. The minute you begin to ask for more is the minute you begin to get more.

The good news is you don't need to find a magical lantern to have a genie grant you your wishes. There are genies all around you. Everyone is a genie. Your friends, your family, your neighbors, and even strangers are genies. You will be surprised at what the people all around you are willing and able to give you. They can help you get what you want through their knowledge, their assistance and their generosity. All you have to do is ask! It is that simple.

In this chapter, I will show you how to ask for anything and everything that you want. You will learn to be bold and courageous in asking for your desires. You will see that you are deserving of your desires and there is no shame or guilt in wanting what you want. You will learn how to ask the right way, ensuring the best chances of getting what you asked for.

The Magic Of Language

We are blessed with the one thing we need so that others will know what our desires are. That tool is language. We have the ability to communicate our wants and desires clearly and precisely. We can describe our requests in finite detail to let others understand exactly what we want. When you go out to a restaurant, you don't just ask the waiter for a plate of food. You look at the menu and make a specific selection.

Think of how hard it must have been in the caveman days before a clear method of speech was invented. How many frustrating loud grunts do you think there were at the dinner table. I mean, what grunt do you use to ask for another helping of Pterodactyl Casserole as opposed to more

Brontosaurus Stew? It is by having a shared language that misunderstandings have been greatly diminished.

With a shared language, people know exactly what I am describing and can give me just that. Would you be surprised if you went to a restaurant and ordered lobster and then received a salad instead? Language has opened up the door to getting exactly what you want. You just need to let the words come out of your mouth, what have you been waiting for? It is time for you to start asking for everything you want. I first realized the power of asking for what you want at a young age. Let me share a story with you that changed my life.

The Curly Haired Bandit

I was eight years old and was hanging out in the local arcade. I didn't have a lot of money, but I was going to treat myself to a few games of pinball. I had four quarters in my pocket and was looking for the next pinball machine I wanted to play. I carefully examined the special ramps and features each one had. I couldn't just rush into such a major decision. I had to look at each game repeatedly. I was determined to get the most bang for my buck.

I was about to put a quarter into one of the machines when I saw a little brunette haired girl walking towards me. She looked to be about my age. She had curly hair, a cute upturned nose and big brown eyes. She was now standing right in front of me and looked directly into my eyes for a few seconds. The silence was broken when she said "Can I have a quarter?" Now without actually knowing it at the time, this was to be a turning point in my life.

As soon as the words left her lips, I was frozen with fear. I was not prepared for her sudden request for my money. I had never been asked for money by a stranger before. I wondered what the proper response was. My eyes darted around the room as I looked for someone who might be able to tell me what I should do. I had straight A's in school, but it was apparent I was woefully unprepared for this situation. There were many thoughts that raced through my head.

Should I give it to her, should I refuse, should I ask her why, should I get something in return? Was she asking for a quarter because she liked me? After what seemed like an unbearable amount of time, I placed a quarter in her hand. I had decided that she must be asking for a quarter because she liked me.

I immediately started to wonder if we would be boyfriend and girlfriend now. Would we spend our afternoons hanging out in the arcade laughing and playing? Would we spend our weekends together getting ice cream and going to the movies? I wondered if her parents will like me. As I stood there daydreaming, she immediately walked away with my quarter in her hand.

I don't remember if she said thank you, or if she said anything at all for that matter. I was heartbroken. Not so much over the loss of my curly haired girlfriend, but I was heartbroken that I just lost one of my quarters. As soon as I watched that little girl walk off, I knew I would never see my quarter again. I realized I had just been robbed. As smooth as that little girl was, I knew that this couldn't have been her first robbery. I thought I should alert the authorities and let them know the curly haired bandit had struck again.

After thinking it over for a few minutes, I came to the conclusion that I wasn't actually robbed, I mean, I did give her the quarter. I then questioned myself as to why I gave her the quarter in the first place. I could have said no.

The amazing thing is she didn't promise me anything for the quarter. She didn't say why she wanted the quarter and she didn't even give me a reason why I should give it to her. She just flat out asked me for it and I gave it to her. What kind of temptress was she that she was able to do this to me? Later, I found out it is just part of a woman's charm and is to be expected at times.

The essence of the story is amazing. This little girl asked me for something with no promise of anything in return and with no hesitation. She had no fear of rejection. She did not mince words with why she wanted it or why I should give it to her. In five simple words, she got what she wanted. "Can I have a quarter?" Could getting what you want really be that easy? Yes, it really is that simple.

Ask For Anything And Everything You Want

Now I know you don't just want an extra quarter in your pocket, but you can apply the same principles to ask for whatever you want. You can ask for big things and small things. You can ask for dates, you can ask for new business, or you can ask for extra lemons for your iced tea. The list is endless of what you can ask for.

Life is a lot more fun when you get more of what you want. And getting what you want is what living a Big Juicy Life is all about. So if it is so easy to get what we want by just asking for it, why do so many of us have difficulty doing it?

It's Ok To Want What You Want

One of the big reasons why we don't ask for what we want is because we are embarrassed. We might feel ashamed of what we truly want and do not want to let anyone else know our desires. We can start judging ourselves on what our wants are and become confused about what we think we should want and what we actually do want. When this happens, you are setting yourself up for a lot of pain and misery.

The truth is there is nothing wrong with wanting whatever you want. We are all unique individuals. It is only natural that you might have different desires than other people. That is one of the beauties of life; we are all free to pursue whatever will make us happy. Variety is the spice of life and it is never truer than when looking at the wide expanse of different desires of all the people in this world.

There is no need for shame or self judgement. You don't even need to explain why you want something. All that matters is that you want it. When you begin to embrace your uniqueness and become comfortable with accepting your desires, you will feel more authentic to whom you truly are. Why go through life having to pretend you are something you are not?

Don't Be Scared

Fear and negative beliefs are the biggest hindrance to us asking for what we want. We might know what we want and are comfortable in our desires, but we are unable to open our mouths and speak the words. It seems like not only did the "cat got your tongue" but he also ran away with it. How did we all get so scared of asking for what we want?

I think we are more brave and courageous when we are younger. We have no problem asking for what we want and there is no self judgement. There is no shame in us asking for an expensive video game system from any family member. We don't get hung up on rejection. We just keep asking until we get what we want. Although a well-placed temper tantrum can also be helpful.

As we grow older, we start developing a sense of self. We become aware of what others might think of us. After a few times being rejected and a few times being embarrassed, many of us have grown more timid than bold. Let's take a look at how to overcome your obstacles in asking for what you want.

Celebrate Rejection

One of the biggest obstacles to asking for what we want is the fear that we will be rejected. The truth is rejection hurts, but most times we make it out to be much worse than it actually is. There is also a hidden beauty of rejection that usually goes unnoticed. I will tell you what it is in just a minute.

One of the most frequent times we open ourselves to possible rejection is when we ask someone out on a date. The reality is we have all been rejected at some time in our life, well, I hope I am not the only one. I have been rejected more times than a porcupine asking out a balloon and more than a turtle at speed dating.

There are many different emotions we can experience when we are rejected. What happens if a person says no to you, do all your insecurities come rushing to the surface? Do you begin to try to find reasons why they said no? You might think it is because you need to lose weight, you need some new clothes, or you might think you are just not attractive.

The reality is there could be 100 reasons why they said no, and the truth is, it doesn't matter what they are. A person saying no to your date request has nothing to do with your intrinsic value. Your worth is never determined by what other people think of you, it is determined only by what you think of you.

When you get rejected, it's no big deal. You're a strong, wonderful, and beautiful being. There's no way that rejection is going to make you second guess your awesomeness. There are so many people who would jump at the chance to get to know you better. And now here is the hidden beauty of rejection.

When you ask someone out and get rejected, celebrate it. Celebrate that you had the courage to go for your heart's desire. Celebrate that you are in control of your destiny. Celebrate that you don't have to wonder what might have been with that person.

It is a terrible way to go through life when you don't go for everything you desire. There is that nagging feeling about imagining what might have been. What if that person was your soulmate? You just let them slip through your fingers by walking away without asking them out. Don't live your life in regret, go for it.

It doesn't have to be just with romantic pursuits, it can be with everything. It is better to ask and get an answer rather than staying silent and wondering what might have been. The world is full of love stories, business startups and lifelong friendships that began with just a simple question.

You Deserve Everything You Desire

We can feel embarrassed or unworthy to ask for so many things. Think about some things that you have difficulty in asking for. Are you too timid to ask to be seated in a booth rather than a table? If your food is not prepared correctly, are you afraid to ask to have it sent back and be corrected?

It wasn't until I was in my 30's that I could feel comfortable in asking for my food to be sent back and be corrected. I have eaten more overcooked steaks than I care to remember. Why did I not just ask to have them remade? I was paying for the food, shouldn't I get it the way I want it? There were two main reasons why I was unable to do it at the time. I didn't want to seem like a pain in the butt and deep down, I had a feeling of unworthiness.

I had a belief that other people's comfort came before my own. I was a people pleaser and put myself second, even to strangers. In the example of the overcooked steaks, I was worried about what people might think of me if I asked to have my food corrected. In my mind, I imagined the waiter saying "Who does this guy think he is? He is a needy, whiney, son of a bitch." Ok, that was a little exaggerated, but you get the idea. I finally realized I don't care what anyone thinks, I am deserving of everything I want and I am going to ask to get it.

The truth is you are deserving of everything you desire. There is no one on this planet that is more deserving than you. There is no need to feel like you are inconveniencing people by asking for what you want. Everyone on earth is in one giant group dance. We are all here to help each other become happier people. The easiest way to do that is to let them know what you are looking for.

Be Bold

It often seems like the hardest part about getting what you want is the ability to work up the courage and confidence to actually ask. This is where your mind starts playing the "What-if" game with you. When you play the "What-if" game, you see yourself asking for what you want and then picture different responses. Usually, your imagination predicts a negative outcome, often with some really terrifying scenarios. It can envision a person laughing at you in slow motion with a distorted voice and then everyone else in the room points at you and starts laughing too. Ok, maybe that is just my visualization.

It is no wonder why we are so hesitant to ask for things, we have scared the hell out of ourselves. Instead of thinking of all the negative things that can happen, think of all the positives that could happen. Picture the outcome where your request is well-received and you get what you want. This will help you generate the courage and confidence for you to be able to ask.

When you play the "What-If" game, always make it have a positive ending. It makes no sense to scare yourself into inaction. Do you want to live in fear or do you want to go for what you want? Be bold, go for it!

One of the benefits of being bold is the understanding that the first one who asks is the one who gets. Think about this example. A mother is handing out chocolate chip cookies to three boys. Each boy gets one cookie and there is one left. One boy asks for the last cookie and gets it. The other two boys feel cheated and wonder why they didn't get an extra cookie. The difference is the other boy asked first.

There are probably many instances in your life of when you witnessed someone who is bold getting rewarded. Have you ever wanted to go out with someone and yet didn't ask? Later, you see them out with a new partner and you think you are a better match for them. You might wonder how come they didn't go out with you instead. You then remember it is because of a minor detail, you never asked them. Don't let happiness pass you by while you stay on the sidelines, ASK!

Create Your Own Opportunities

In most areas of our life, we have been conditioned to respond to opportunities instead of creating them for ourselves. We tend to be reactive with opportunities rather than proactive. When you understand the true power of asking, you can create new opportunities out of thin air. You do not have to wait for opportunities to present themselves, you make them yourself.

You can create new jobs and positions for yourself that didn't exist before. You can learn from people who weren't even looking to teach someone. You don't have to wait for something to go on sale, you can ask for a better deal anytime you want. When you understand this amazing power you have, you will always be at the right place at the right time.

Let me give you an example. You don't have to wait to see a help wanted sign in the window before you go into a business and apply for a job. You might walk in and ask the owner if she could use anymore help. The owner might suddenly realize she does need more help, and there you are. Congratulations, you just created a job for yourself! Your friends might ask you how you got the job, they didn't know the establishment was hiring. Well, they weren't until you asked them.

You can also use this principle when you are looking to be more fulfilled at your current job. I was once working at a restaurant which was only open at night. It was a beautiful place with a big stage, a huge flat screen TV, and a great sound system. I thought it would be a great place to have corporate functions during the day. I thought I would be able to book the restaurant for corporate meetings and pitched the idea to the restaurant owners. They liked the idea and I created a position for myself as a part time banquet coordinator.

You will be amazed at how well this works in all areas of your life. Another opportunity you can create is the ability to learn from others. You can ask for knowledge from people in all types of settings. Most people appreciate someone who is interested in what they do and would love to help you. They would've been glad to help anybody who wanted it, but nobody ever asked before.

When you see somebody doing something admirable, you can ask them to show you how to do it. You can walk up to someone and say, "Wow, that was amazing how you did that, can you show me how to do it?" It could be a dance move, a public presentation, or how to throw a dart without injuring the bartender at your local bar.

It is really limitless what you can ask for people to show you. Once you realize that everyone around you is a teacher, then you can quickly gain more knowledge than ever before. And not only are you gaining knowledge, you are making new friends and associations that can lead to something more in the future.

It might feel a little awkward at first to be so bold, but once you see how well it works, the world will become your playground. You will look at people in a different way. You will uncover all the hidden genies that are all around you. You will have more opportunities than other people.

Ask The Right Way

The way you ask for things is just as important as what you're asking for. It is important to ask in the best way possible in order to maximize your chances of getting what you want. Many people start off asking for things in a negative or inappropriate way. Words are very powerful and definitely affect peoples' level of cooperation.

It is never a good idea to ask for something by beginning your request with phrases like "give me", "get me", or "bring me". If you are beginning your requests in that form, it immediately gives people the impression that you are greedy or unappreciative. A much better way of beginning your requests are by using the phrases "can I", "may I", or "is it possible".

Another important aspect of asking the right way is don't use negative leading questions. A negative leading question is one where you do not anticipate your request being granted and you make it easy for the response to be no. Let me give you an example. If you wanted to ask someone out on a date, a negative leading question would be "You wouldn't want to go out with me this weekend, would you?"

Even though you are asking them to go out with you, your lack of confidence will come through and your phrasing will make it easy for them to say no. It sets the tone for your request to be easily denied. When you are asking with negative leading questions, you are telling people you don't believe you deserve it and you will be surprised if they say yes. Although it might feel easier to put questions in this way to lessen any possible pain from rejection, it is counterproductive.

Just as you can make it easier for people to say no, you can also make it easier for people to say yes. You can do this by using positive leading questions. A positive leading question already assumes the answer will be yes and goes straight to the next question. Here is an example of a positive leading question, "I would love to go out with you this weekend, would Friday or Saturday be better for you?"

In that example, you did not ask whether or not they would like to go out with you. You are automatically assuming their answer will be yes. You have jumped ahead to the next logical question you would ask if they agreed to go out with you this weekend. They just have to decide what day is best for them.

If you are in sales, you will be amazed at how effective positive leading questions can be. Instead of asking someone if they would like to purchase a balloon, you can ask them if they want to buy a red balloon or a blue balloon. You are already assuming they are going to buy a balloon, they just have to tell you what color they would like.

You will be surprised at how easy it is to upsell customers in the business world using this technique. If you give people only two choices, they often internalize that those are the only options they have to choose from. That is not the case, but it is more difficult to say no when that is not one of the choices that you are given.

Here is an example of a positive leading question upsell. I remember going to my local fast food restaurant and ordering a combo meal that was advertised on TV. It came with a cheeseburger, small french fries and a small drink. The cashier asked me if I would like a medium or a large combo. Without giving it too much thought, I asked for a medium. As I sat down and started eating my meal, it dawned on me I had been upsold. The combo meal that was advertised came with small fries and a small drink. The medium or large combo would be a higher price. I would have been fine with the small combo, but because the cashier did not include that as one of my choices, I picked the smaller of the two. I smiled to myself and knew that I had fallen victim to the power of the positive leading question.

Although positive leading questions can be helpful, do not overuse them. They are not appropriate in all situations. They can cause people to believe that you are trying to trick them or manipulate them, and nobody likes that. Experiment with them to see when their use is appropriate for you.

Ask From The Heart

One of the keys to getting what you want is to ask from a heartfelt space. There are many things that you could get in this world just by asking for them, but don't take advantage of people's generosity. Always make sure you have good intentions when asking things of others.

When you come from a heartfelt space when you ask for things, people will be able to sense your sincerity and be more willing to help. The person giving you something will not feel like they have been taken advantage of or manipulated.

When you ask with humility and appreciation in advance for what you are requesting, the person gives freely and openly without any regret. Even if they deny your request, they will appreciate and respect the way and manner that you asked.

Some people question what the benefit is to those who help others. It seems like it is a one sided exchange. The truth is that by helping others, they are also receiving something in return. It feels good knowing you were able to bring more happiness into another's life. When you see the beauty of giving, it can also let you see that asking for what you want is not so selfish after all.

Ask More Than Once

When we ask for something and the answer is no, many of us will accept that as the final answer and move on. In some cases, that is the appropriate action, but in many cases you could ask again. You might feel like there is no reason to ask again, because they already said no. But you are missing out on the dynamic motion of life.

Life is so dynamic. There are so many things that change daily or even hourly. Our moods, our situations, and our desires are constantly changing. What was true just a few minutes ago, is no longer true.

Has anyone ever asked you if you wanted to go have lunch together and you said no, because you weren't hungry? What would happen if that same person came up to you an hour later and asked you again? You might say yes this time. You may have gotten hungry since the last time they asked.

This ever-changing dynamic applies to all areas of your desires. If you asked for a raise last month and was turned down, maybe you could ask again this month. You know the sales team exceeded its sales target this quarter. That might have changed the company's position on raises.

If you asked someone out last month and they said no, maybe they needed more time to get over a previous partner. Maybe this month they have decided they are ready to start dating again. When you ask again this time, you are in the right place and the right time to get a yes.

The point is do not be afraid to ask more than once for something you still desire. Persistence can be rewarded. Be aware though there is a big difference between being persistent and being hounded or becoming a stalker. Always be respectful when asking a second time and do not be negative or disgruntled if the answer is no again. Repeated asking does not guarantee an eventual yes.

Be Clear

One of the big mistakes we make is that we are not clear in what we are asking for. Have you ever been disappointed with what you received when you weren't perfectly clear? Maybe you asked for a new furry pet for your birthday, and you got a gerbil instead of a dog.

Sometimes we have an unrealistic expectation that others should be mind readers. The good news is people don't have to possess super powers to know what you are longing for; instead you can just tell them exactly what you want.

It is always best to be as clear as possible about what you want. You can save yourself a lot of frustration by being able to be specific with your requests. Don't beat around the bush, don't leave innuendos, and don't count on others to fill in the blanks of what they think you are looking for. Be upfront and honest. Be bold and believe that you are worthy and deserving. Do not be afraid to fully commit to what your desire actually is. Don't start to backpedal or soften your desire if you get nervous. Articulate fully and clearly what your desire is. You know what you want, ask for it!

Be Grateful

There are so many things that you have asked for and received, have you shown appreciation and gratitude for all those gifts? Are you quick to give thanks to others that help you? Asking for things and getting them is great, but you should always remember to thank those who help you. Showing gratitude and appreciation is also a part of making sure your heart was in the right place.

Sometimes we get wrapped up in the excitement of getting what we asked for that we forget to give thanks. It is important to make time, even if it is at a later date to show appreciation to the people that have helped you. Thanking others is a way of giving back and showing them there is mutual respect and an understanding that you cannot do everything on your own.

When you are grateful to others for their help, you are recognizing the beauty of their hearts in helping you. Many times when you are grateful, you naturally become more giving also. It feels good to help others, especially when you realize how impactful it was that someone was there to help you at an important time in your life. Once you realize the amazing ability we all have to help each other, the world can become a much more beautiful and loving place. That is what the term "pay it forward" means. Help others and be grateful and it will be a chain reaction that can change the world.

Chapter Summary

- **You can get what you want by simply asking for it**

- **It is ok to want whatever you desire without shame or guilt**

- **Do not be afraid of rejection**

- **You deserve everything you desire**

- **Create your own opportunities by asking for things proactively instead of reactively**

- **Ask for what you want from the heart and be grateful when receiving**

Action Plan

Make a list of some small things you have trouble asking for.

Example: I have trouble asking for my food to be sent back and be corrected.

1. _____

2. _____

3. _____

4. _____

5. _____

Make a list of some big things you would like to ask for.

Example: I would like to ask for a raise.

1. _____

2. _____

3. _____

4. _____

5. _____

Write down the reasons why you haven't asked for what you want.

Example: I am afraid I will be rejected.

1. _____

2. _____

3. _____

4. _____

5. _____

It is now time to start overcoming your fear of rejection, being embarrassed or any other reasons you might have written down. You are missing out on so many things you desire by living in fear. Remember, the one that asks is the one that gets.

It is time to start taking chances and asking for things that you want. Sure, you might get rejected, but who cares. If you get rejected, that is not a reflection on your self-worth. You are a strong, confident and wonderful being and someone saying "no" isn't going to change that.

Be bold and begin experimenting with asking for things. You will be surprised at how fun it can be. You can start by asking for some of the small things on your list from the previous page. Once you are successful in getting some of your small desires granted, it will give you the confidence to ask for bigger things. Now pick a few of your bigger desires from your list and go for it!

It is important to be thankful for people who have made your desires come true. Take a look in your life and see if there are people you forgot to thank for helping you. It could be recent or some time ago. Make a list of people you will thank in the next few days.

1. _____

2. _____

3. _____

4. _____

5. _____

It is great to see the magic of how people can help make all your dreams come true, but is important to show appreciation and give thanks. And don't forget to be a genie for other people too. We are all here to make each other's lives better!

Daily Action:

1. Be bold in asking for what you want.

2. Ask for everything in a polite way.

3. Ask from the heart and show appreciation for people's help.

4. Engage all the genies around you to make your life better.

5. Be a genie for other people also.

"Money is a terrible master but an excellent servant."

- P.T. Barnum

Chapter 11: The Real Value Of Money

When most people think about being happy and successful, they inevitably think about how much money they have. In our society, we are led to believe the more money that we have, the happier we will be. In a similar belief, we are taught that the more money we have, the more successful we are.

The truth is having lots of money does not guarantee happiness; likewise, success is not determined by how much money you have. We all have different ideas of what makes someone successful. You might believe that someone who has a great relationship with their partner is more successful than a person with a lot of money. There are no right or wrong versions of success. The important point to remember is success is not just about how much money you have.

There is no doubt that money is valuable and can add to your life's enjoyment, but we have been conditioned on using it mainly to buy material goods. The fact is there are other things you can spend your money on that will bring you more opportunities for love, joy and success than material goods could ever offer.

In this chapter we are going to talk about why we have been fooled into believing that money is the key to our happiness and success. I am going to show you the truth about money and its real purpose. You will also learn how to use money to have more happiness and love in your life.

Why Are We Obsessed With Money

One of the reasons we are so obsessed with money is that we think it is the path to everything we desire. The attainment of more money seems like a sure fire way to have all the love, joy and success you deserve. It is easy to look around and see examples of where we got these beliefs.

There are TV ads, infomercials and music videos showing people drinking champagne in their million dollar mansions or posing in front of their Italian sports car. They are surrounded by beautiful people and are always having a party. After seeing all that, how could you not be convinced that lots of money is the key to happiness?

The belief that having lots of money is a guaranteed way to have "the good life" can consume people. People can become focused on getting more money and nothing else. They miss out on all the joy and happiness that is right in front of them. There is also a feeling of impatience in attaining more money. After all, who wants to wait to feel better and have the life of their dreams? I want it, and I want it now! I sound like the spoiled little rich girl from Willy Wonka.

Our society is into instant gratification and shortcuts. We are always looking for ways we can make money faster and easier. We hear stories of people hitting it big with one great investment or one amazing business opportunity. These stories fuel our hunger to find an opportunity for ourselves. We start looking for our big break to come so we can hit it big too. Unfortunately, many of those opportunities turn out to be fool's gold and we end up losing money instead of making money. Let me share an experience with you of when I learned a painful lesson about trying to take a shortcut.

My $10,000 Lesson

I don't come from a wealthy family. We weren't poor by any stretch but our family lived within our means. I knew the importance of being frugal. I was self-reliant and began working at the age of 15. By the time I was 22 years old, I had been a police officer for three years and was saving money to move out of my mom's house and buy a condominium.

My plan was to set myself up for a good financial future. I had already learned to invest in stocks and I thought I had a good handle on making the most of my money. I even paid my credit cards off in full each month to avoid paying interest. I was ready to start buying property and begin building my financial empire. I was going to be the next Donald Trump.

One day a police sergeant I knew told me about a great investment opportunity. He told me that his friend had a business where they would buy property that was undervalued and then sell it to companies at a high profit. If I invested, my money would be used as upfront money to buy the properties and then be returned after a short period of time with 18% interest.

The premise sounded believable to me. I even met the man who owned the company. He answered my questions and I felt reassured. Also, I figured that since it was someone I knew and trusted that was getting me involved, it must be legitimate. Plus, the fact that he was a police sergeant also made me feel more comfortable.

I thought it through and it seemed like a good idea. I figured it would be a great way to accelerate my goal of buying a condominium. I invested $10,000 in cash and received a notarized letter in return. The letter stated I would be receiving my original $10,000 back along with 18 percent interest in 6 months.

About 4 months later, I received some heartbreaking news. The sergeant informed me that the real estate venture was a scam and I had just lost all of my money. I couldn't believe what I was hearing. How the hell could something like this happen to me?

I was in shock. In one quick moment, my $10,000 was gone and there wasn't a damn thing I could do about it. Several other people I knew also lost money in the same scam. There were also other people who had heard about the opportunity, but for some reason decided not to invest. They say that misery loves company, but I wanted to turn back time and have a do-over. I wanted to be in the company of the people who did not invest. They weren't the ones kicking themselves in the ass for being so stupid.

As I began to process what happened, I realized that the $10,000 I just lost was over half of my net salary for a year. In one fateful decision, I had basically worked six months for nothing. That was a bitter pill to swallow.

I had been so frugal and careful with my money in the past and I just blew 10 grand on nothing. I imagined all the things that I could have bought with that money. I could have gone on several vacations, bought a new motorcycle, or bought a new Jet Ski. The list went on and on. It felt like torture thinking of all the things I could have done with the money I had lost.

I analyzed my poor decision a thousand times, each time trying to find reasons to soften the blow of losing all that money. I realized I had let greed overpower my sense of rational decision making. In hindsight, it was easy to see what factors I held onto rather than see the danger. I felt safe with my decision because some of my friends had also invested money. I believed there was safety in numbers. I also trusted a police sergeant in thinking he would not be involved with an illegal Ponzi scheme.

The monetary loss was devastating. I was sick to my stomach for months. It was hard to think about anything else. It was also a huge blow to my plan of buying a condominium anytime soon. Even though my life went on, it was heart wrenching for many years trying to forgive myself for being so stupid. Each night before I went to sleep, it seemed like I could not help but remember how I lost all that money. It was like a nightmare that just kept repeating.

It was the hardest financial lesson I ever learned and it happened to me at a young age. I was very fortunate that I still had a job and a steady source of income that allowed me to start saving money again. I eventually learned to forgive myself for losing all that money, although I still daydream sometimes about what I would do with an extra $10,000.

Beware The Get Rich Quick Scheme

The belief that lots of money will bring you happiness is quite alluring. So what could be wrong with getting more of it as quick and easy as possible? This is where greed can corrupt your logical thinking. You can begin to convince yourself that for once, you are in the right place at the right time, and this is your golden opportunity. You start to be more afraid of missing your big opportunity rather than looking at the situation from a rational standpoint. Suddenly it sounds believable that the Nigerian Prince has selected you to inherit his fortune.

Many of the scams seem silly when you are not involved with them. You might think how could people be so gullible? If you have lost money in a scam, take comfort in knowing you are not alone. We all have been duped at some time in our lives. The important thing is you don't make the same mistake twice.

The truth is there are many legitimate opportunities to make money out there. It is important to understand that any investment to make money involves risk though. Research and knowledge are the best tools you can use to make the best decisions with your money. Beware of the impulse to talk yourself into a bad investment though. If it seems too good to be true, it probably is.

Money Is Good

Money can get a bad rap sometimes; it has even been called the root of all evil. That sounds a little harsh don't you think? I can think of several things more evil than money; alarm clocks, cheese fries, and Barry Manilow come to mind.

The truth is money is not bad. Money is good. The reason why money is good is because of what it can do for you. It can help bring you happiness. The real purpose of money is to add happiness to your life.

There are so many different ways that you can spend your money to make your life more fulfilled. Many people incorrectly believe that buying material goods will fill all their emotional needs. How did we become so brainwashed into thinking that material goods will satisfy our needs for acceptance, security, and love? It is because we are heavily influenced by advertisements and commercials.

Don't Believe The Hype

We are conditioned to think that having certain material goods will give us the love, joy, and success we have been looking for. We are bombarded by persuasive commercials and ads on a daily basis. The way that they can relate a material good to having love and success would be comical if they weren't so damn effective.

The advertising companies know what we are truly looking for. We are not after material goods; we are looking for romance, excitement and prestige. They convince us that by wearing their perfume/cologne, you will be making out with a supermodel on the coast of Italy. If you buy their car, you will be racing down the highway, leaving all your troubles behind. By wearing their diver's watch that is waterproof to 4000 meters, the world will know you have made it.

It is difficult to resist the temptation of their messages. After seeing all of those ads, I have a drawer full of expensive cologne and not once has a supermodel invited me to Italy. My turbocharged sports car still gets stuck in traffic jams when I leave work, and I wear my divers watch in the bathtub to try and make me feel better about its purchase.

It does feel good to have nice things, but what if I told you can use your money to get more happiness in a different way?

I want you to think about some of the most enjoyable times of your life. What were you doing? Were you sitting in your 5-bedroom house on your Italian leather couch watching your big-screen TV? Was it looking out in the driveway and seeing your luxury sports car? Was it checking the time on your diamond crusted watch? Or did your most enjoyable moments happen when you were able to experience something?

Was it a romantic dinner, overlooking the city with your partner? Was it jumping out of an airplane with your friends to celebrate your birthday? Or perhaps it was watching your children squeal with delight as they met their favorite princess at an amusement park? The truth is that experiences can bring you more happiness than any material thing ever could.

Spending Money On Experiences

I don't know if you know this, but you can't take your money with you when you die. That also means you can't take any material possessions with you. If we can't take any material goods with us, then why focus on accumulating more of them. Remember, it is not true that whoever dies with the most toys, wins.

Even though a vacation or tickets to a concert might seem fleeting, the truth is those experiences can stay with you for a lifetime. I still remember seeing Phantom of the Opera on Broadway in New York. It was one of the best nights of my life. It does not matter how much time passes, the memories I have from that night are priceless. There is nothing I could have spent that money on that would have brought me as much joy as that magical evening.

Having new experiences opens you up to doing new things, seeing new places and meeting new people. It is through those interactions that will give you more opportunities to find love, joy and success. Think about some of your past experiences that illustrate this point. Have you ever met a new lover or friend while you were on vacation? Have you ever laughed out loud in a comedy club? Did you make more money after you received your degree? These are all things material goods cannot offer you.

There are so many different experiences that money can buy. You might be surprised at some you may not have considered before. It is time to open your eyes and see the many wonderful opportunities that are waiting for you. Spending money is a personal issue and the good news is you get to choose which experiences you find most valuable. Let's take a look at some options for you.

Traveling

Traveling has always been a strong desire for most people. There is nothing quite as exhilarating as seeing something for the first time. Whether it is a giraffe at the zoo, a sunset on a tropical beach, or a snow covered mountain vista. The world is filled with an endless supply of new sights just waiting to be seen.

Traveling to different destinations is not just about what you will see. It is also about meeting new people and seeing how they live. It can be life changing to see how the way you live contrasts with other people's lives. It can foster a deep sense of appreciation for all that you have in your life.

Instead of just thinking about typical vacation destinations, you might want to branch out and look for more joy by choosing different experiences than you normally would. Instead of taking a tropical cruise and getting tipsy on Pina-coladas, how about a trip to see the rain forest? You can learn about how this precious resource is being destroyed and it might inspire you to get involved. Or how about taking a trip where you can learn a new skill or activity? How do surfing lessons in Hawaii sound?

There are also opportunities to make a difference in others' lives while you are traveling. There are programs where you can go to different countries and help the people who live there. You might be able to help build new schools, help with medical treatment, or just be a friendly face to teach them a little English. Think about how great it would be to see a new country and be able to make a difference in someone else's life while there. There is no doubt you would make memories that will last a lifetime.

Educational Experiences

People often overlook the value of learning something new. As soon as we get our high school diploma, we swear off reading books and dread the idea of ever stepping foot in a classroom again. The truth is learning is fun, especially when you get to choose what you want to study. There are literally millions of different subjects you can discover. It feels good putting your brain to good use, rather than using it to figure out which piece of candy to crush on your smartphone.

Educational experiences don't just have to be about attending college or an organized school. You can go to seminars and workshops. You can also learn anything you can think of from online lessons. Never before has information been as accessible and available as it is today.

Try spending some of your money on educational experiences and see how it feels. Instead of buying the newest video game or a new pair of high heels, sign up to take a class at your local college. I am sure you will find something that interests you. You might be surprised at how much fun you will have. Not only that, but you will meet new people, make new friendships, and have new opportunities to continue advancing in your area of interest.

Your new educational pursuits might also allow you to translate your new knowledge into business opportunities. Many times people end up making money with their hobbies. What started out as a personal interest became a new source of income. How great is that?

Charity

The value of giving to others is often overlooked by many people. Some people might question what joy could come from them giving something and not getting anything in return. Wouldn't my money be better spent on something that will benefit me? This is one of the biggest misconceptions about charity.

The truth is giving to someone else is one of the best gifts you could ever give to yourself. There is something magical that happens when you realize you are able to make a difference in someone else's life. You feel powerful, you feel humble and you feel joy. The first time you see a smiling face on an impoverished child that you have bought a brand new toy for, it can melt your heart.

The beauty of spending your money on others is it doesn't have to be extravagant or excessive to make a difference. Just a small gift or a small amount of money can brighten someone else's life.

There are many different ways you can spend money to help others besides just people. If you are looking for a quick boost of happiness in your life, buy a bag of dog food and take it to your local animal shelter. I am sure they will appreciate it and you can spend some time petting and playing with the animals you just bought the food for. How would it make you feel knowing that you are helping those dogs stay healthy and nourished until they find their new home?

Treat Yourself

For some strange reason, it is often easier to treat others nicer than we treat ourselves. You might have no problem buying gift certificates for friends to go to the day spa, but when was the last time you treated yourself to a massage? It is time to put yourself first on the pampering list.

When was the last time you showed yourself some love by spending money on you? Sure there are other things that might seem more practical to spend your money on, but what is more important than you feeling good? The truth is you deserve to feel happy and spending money on yourself to feel better is money well spent.

There are so many experiences that can make you feel pampered and loved. Anything that can make you feel better; emotionally, spiritually or physically is worth it. You might consider trying some new experiences. Perhaps you can book a Reiki session, hire a personal trainer, or let a life coach help you achieve your goals.

Happiness Is Free

Money's real purpose is to make you happy. Notice though, that I didn't say that it is the only way to find happiness. The beautiful thing about happiness, love and success is that it doesn't have to cost anything at all. Despite what TV commercials and advertisements tell you, you can have an awesome life without a big mansion and a speedboat.

Let's talk about some of the different ways you can find joy without spending any money.

Traveling to foreign countries is amazing, but so is checking out your local parks and attractions. I bet there is a nearby free museum you have never been to. Even if you have been to your local attractions before, experience it again like it was your first time. Try and notice things you have never seen before. You can bring a camera and take some interesting photos to show your friends or post online.

If money is an issue and you feel like being pampered, you can barter and trade services with friends and family. Remember the old adage of "If you scratch my back, I'll scratch yours?" You could even invite some friends over and take turns massaging each other's backs. Add some wine and a little music and you have a massage party on your hands.

When it comes to charity, you don't just have to donate money. You can donate your time, knowledge and resources. These are just as valuable as any financial donation you can make. They can still give you that wonderful feeling of knowing you are helping others. That feeling is priceless.

If you desire educational experiences but don't have the money, you can volunteer to help out at a seminar in exchange for attending it. You can contact your local community college and see what free programs they are offering. You can ask friends, family and even strangers to teach you something they have expertise in. Most people enjoy sharing their wisdom and experience.

I hope by now you see that money is not the root of all happiness. It is just a tool that can add new layers and flavors to your life journey. Try to use your money in new ways that will open the door to more love, joy and success.

Chapter Summary

- Having a lot of money does not guarantee happiness

- Do not be obsessed with the pursuit of money

- Money is good

- Money's purpose is to help make you happy

- Experiences can bring you more happiness than material things

- Having more experiences will give you more opportunities to find love, joy and success

- Try new ways of spending your money, including education, travel and charity

- You do not need money to have love, joy and success

Action Plan

Make a list of some of the best times of your life.

1. _____

2. _____

3. _____

4. _____

5. _____

6. _____

7. _____

Were all of them experiences? Did you include any times when you bought something? Chances are the best times of your life were when you experienced something and not when you bought something.

Focus on spending your money on experiences rather than material goods. It is by having more experiences that will give you more opportunities to find love, joy and success.

Spending money on experiences is what can bring you the most joy. List some new experiences you would like to try. Come up with at least one experience in each category that you commit to doing.

Charity_____

Travel_____

Education_____

Pampering/Self Love_____

You might be surprised at what experiences made you feel happy. Once you see what experiences brought you the most joy, you can focus on spending more of your money in those particular areas.

Take a look at what you spend your money on. Keep a journal on where your money goes. It can be quite an eye opener to see how much money you are spending in different areas. Do you spend $5 a day buying a cup of coffee at your local coffee shop? That is $1,300 a year just spent on cups of coffee. Perhaps you can make a budget and cut back on your coffee purchases and use that money for a vacation.

Increase your knowledge of the different ways you can make more money. Learn about the stock market and understand the different ways you can invest your money. Learn what mutual funds are and see if they are right for you. Start a retirement account on your own or see what is available through your place of employment.

Daily Action:

1. Treat yourself nice, but be wise with your money.

2. Make a budget and stick to it.

3. Buy things when they are on sale.

4. Do not be swayed into believing that you need lots of money to be happy.

5. Look for free events and activities that are available in your local area.

6. Spend more of your money on experiences rather than material goods.

"You don't stop laughing because you grow old. You grow old because you stop laughing."

- Michael Pritchard

Chapter 12: Laugh Dammit

In today's world, there is a lot to be stressed out about; your job, your health, and the rising cost of Fruit Loops. Wouldn't it be great if there was something you could do on a daily basis that would make you feel better? Wouldn't it be great if there was an all-natural stress reliever that didn't cost anything and had no negative side effects? I've got great news for you. There is something you can do that will fill the bill for all those requirements. It is your ability to laugh.

Laughing benefits your mind, body, and spirit. It is the all-natural wonder drug for whatever ails you. If you are feeling sad, laughing releases endorphins into your blood stream that make you feel better. Endorphins are neurotransmitters your body produces which can immediately make you feel less stressed and can even temporarily alleviate pain. You can tap into your endorphins as much as you like and the good news is you won't have to check into a rehab afterwards.

Laughing has many other benefits also. It can strengthen your immune system, which means you will get sick less often and have a higher resistance to the nasty stuff lingering in your office watercooler. Laughter also helps keep your heart healthy by improving the function of your blood vessels and increases blood flow. Who knew laughter was so beneficial to your health.

Laughter is also the common language of everyone around you. It is the universal "ice-breaker." When people are laughing, they are more at ease and more likely to be open to forge deeper relationships, whether it is on a personal or a business level.

When you are wrapped up in a loop of painful emotions, laughter can help you break your negative train of thought. It can shock your system into being able to think about something more positive. Having a humorous perspective can also help you from overreacting to everything around you.

Now that you are excited about bringing more laughter into your life, let's get started. In this chapter, I'm going to show you how to include more laughter into your daily life. It is very easy to do. With a simple change in focus to find more humor, you will be laughing daily. One of the best ways to find laughter is by remembering funny or embarrassing events that have happened in your life.

Tell Me A Funny Story

One of the ways that you can start including more laughter in your life is to remember your own humorous incidents. You can share your stories when something funny happened to you. Maybe it was an embarrassing moment or a time when something didn't go exactly as planned. You might not want to share the story of where your felony bank robbery went wrong, but I am sure you have some funny stories that people would love to hear.

Being able to laugh at yourself can lessen the sting of any possible pain or disappointment in embarrassing situations. It also can relieve the pressure you might put on yourself to be perfect. Once you start seeing the humor in your experiences, suddenly they do not seem like a big deal anymore.

When you share your stories with other people, they can let their guard down and be more comfortable around you. Once you show people that you are being authentic and vulnerable, they will find it easier to open up to you. This dynamic allows for a strong bond to begin to develop. Now let me start bonding with you by sharing a couple funny stories of when things did not go as planned for me.

My Big Drum Audition

Like many children, I wanted to play an instrument in elementary school. My mother talked me out of learning the tuba and said I could learn to play the drums instead. I learned to play a single drum called the snare drum. It wasn't as flashy as the tuba, but I could still make some loud noise so I was satisfied.

I continued playing the drums into middle school. By then, I could read rudimentary sheet music and had gotten pretty good. I actually had a solo on one of our songs during my seventh grade recital. I was so nervous the night of my big solo. I think it was the first time I realized the value of antiperspirant/deodorant.

My music teacher was a wonderful woman. She believed in me and she encouraged me to audition for the state band. I thought that it would be a good idea, why should I hide my amazing drumming talent from the rest of the world? The one thing that was stopping me though was I did not have money for the application fee. When I told her I didn't have the money, she generously offered it to me. That lady was a saint.

My audition date arrived and I walked into the state concert hall. The room was full of the instructors and judges that would be listening to my audition. I sat down in front of the snare drum and they presented me with the sheet music I was to be playing. I took one look at the sheet music and my stomach sank into my socks. I immediately knew I was in trouble.

I had never seen sheet music like that before in my life. It looked like hieroglyphics to me. The notes were so close together, they had squiggles above and below some of the notes, and it seemed like there were bars connecting the lines scattered everywhere. There was no way I was going to be able to play this.

Not only was there no way I was going to be able to play this, there was no way I was going to even come close to playing anything even remotely resembling it. I became fully aware that this was going to be epic, epically bad.

In an effort to avoid embarrassing myself, I thought about causing a scene and kicking over the drum and storming out – I heard that's what rock legends do from time to time – maybe they would think that the music was beneath me and an insult to my playing ability. Right before I was ready to kick over the drum and leave, I thought of something else.

At that moment, I realized that my music teacher was no saint. She clearly was a sadist. How could she send me into this musical slaughter so unprepared? What was she thinking? She must have known this sheet music was beyond my capability. My sense of love and compassion towards my music teacher had turned to anger and loathing. While I was planning out vengeance in my mind, I realized I was still sitting in front of the judges.

I took a deep breath and thought the show must go on. Plus, the quicker I bang these sticks, the quicker I can get the hell out of there. I started my audition with an amazing display of my fine drumming talent. Let me describe what my fine drumming talent actually consisted of. Picture a monkey randomly banging on a drum, all the while having a ridiculous smile on his face. The only difference was I wasn't smiling.

I banged on that drum like I was trying to swat flies that had landed on the drumhead. There was no timing or tempo involved. As I continued, I had no concept of how long I was playing and where I should be if I had actually been playing the sheet music. Suddenly and without warning, I brought this musical masterpiece to an end. I ended my audition with a loud crisp note on the snare drum. It was like an exclamation point to my fearless and selfless display of my musical incompetence.

I kept my head down and couldn't bear to look up at the people in front of me. I thought they might be laughing. There was no laughter, but there was a sense of sadness for the drumming profession as a whole. I wanted to apologize to them for wasting their time. The judges were polite and said thank you. I was just glad they didn't take my drumsticks and break them in half and hand them back to me.

As I walked out into the hall, I was in shock. What the hell just happened in there? Boy, was that a disaster. I realized I was really not that good at playing the drums after all. It was a good thing I wasn't banking on making a career out of my drumming talent. Maybe I could try the tuba instead.

Later that evening, I shared what had happened with my family. As I reenacted my drum solo, we all laughed heartily. I did my best monkey impression while banging on an imaginary drum. While my mom was still laughing, I asked her if I could learn to play the tuba. She abruptly stopped laughing and said no. It was the end of my music career.

I had failed miserably, but it was ok. It was not the end of the world. It made me feel better to find the humor in the situation rather than to beat myself up over it. The good news is I eventually forgave my music teacher and will forever be grateful for her support and encouragement.

It's easy to take life too seriously. It does not matter how old you are or where you are in your life, there will always be things that don't work out as planned. The key is to learn to laugh at yourself. We all make mistakes. We all do dumb and silly things. We all have slipped and fell in front of people.

My Lesson In Gravity

I was in college and had just pulled into the school parking lot. It was a winter day and the parking lot was a sheet of ice. I got out of my car with what seemed like a library's worth of books in my arms. I took a few steps away from my car and that's when it happened.

My feet started to slide out from underneath me. I tried to fight it by putting one foot quickly in front of another. It looked like one of those cartoon scenes when the character is running in place but not going anywhere. I could almost hear the silly cartoon music in my head as I quickly surmised I was about to learn a painful lesson about the law of gravity.

My feet could no longer move fast enough to keep me upright and with one big whoosh, my books flew up into the air. As my books went up, I went down and landed hard on the iced pavement. I lay there for a moment and then began a mental check to see if any of my bones had been broken. Ok, I can wiggle my toes and I can still feel my fingers. I think I am good.

I stayed on the ground for a few seconds hoping that nobody saw me fall. I figured if I lay there long enough, I would freeze to death and not have to see anyone laughing at me. As I was eagerly waiting to lose consciousness, I looked up and saw a classmate laughing hysterically.

He came over to me and helped me up from the pavement. We both gathered up my books and I brushed myself off. He said "Man, that was pretty funny, I am glad you are not hurt." As we both walked to class together, he proceeded to tell me his story about when he slipped on the diving board and did a belly flop into the community pool. We both laughed and decided it wasn't a big deal that we fell. From that day forward, we ended up becoming good friends. It was because I was able to laugh at myself that I turned a negative event into a positive one.

There Is Laughter Everywhere

There's a saying that some people can't see the forest through the trees. What that means is that they're missing something that's right in front of them. It is no different when people say that there's nothing funny in their lives.

Our lives are filled with endless opportunities to laugh at something. Just like there is beauty all around you, there are things that are funny everywhere. You just need to put on a pair of funny glasses. I'm not talking about the fake nose and mustache glasses, just an invisible pair of glasses that will let you see humor all around you.

Have you ever seen children at play? Don't they do and say the funniest things? The amazing thing is that they're not trying to be funny, but it's absolutely hilarious. When they are running around and bumping into each other, it looks like they are doing a perfectly rehearsed slapstick routine. And you couldn't write a script any funnier than some kids conversations with each other – children have no filter – they say the first thing that comes into their minds. Their openness is quite refreshing and funny.

Do you have a pet at home? How many funny things does your pet do on a daily basis? My dog would play a game where I would give her a tennis ball and she would immediately knock it underneath the couch with her nose so that she could no longer reach it. She would then bark frantically at me to get her the ball. After I retrieved the ball for her, she would immediately knock it underneath the couch again and start barking at me to get it. This would go on for hours it seemed. I could not help but laugh at her and enjoy the playful moments we shared together. It could always brighten my mood no matter what was going on in my life.

Funny Media

What are some of your favorite funny movies? The great thing about funny movies is that they don't lose their ability to make you laugh even if you've seen it before. The same is true for other comedy media. Funny media is the gift that keeps giving; it's like a lollipop that never loses its flavor.

There are all types of media available that you can use to bring more laughter into your life. They could be movies, videos, books, comics, recordings, etc. You do not even need to buy them. Many of them you can find on the internet and are free. You have access to an immense comedy library 24 hours a day, seven days a week. You don't even have to leave the house.

Try to incorporate all different types of funny media into your daily life. Let me give you an example. Download audio of comedians performing their best material and listen to it on the way to work. Your boss will love it when he sees a smile on your face when you walk in the door. He might actually think you enjoy working there.

Live Comedy

One of the best ways to bring more laughter into your life is to go to a comedy club. Instead of going to see the latest slasher movie, consider making it a night of humor instead of a night of horror. The good news is you will dream about giggling unicorns instead of getting chased all night with a butcher knife.

Something pretty cool happens as soon as you step foot into a comedy club. You start to feel a little more relaxed because you know what is coming. You know you are going to laugh. The anticipation feels good and you can't wait to see what happens next. It's the opposite effect of when you walk into the dentist's office.

Funny Activities

Another great way to add more laughter into your life is by spending time with your friends doing certain activities. There are many activities that lend themselves to producing funny moments. Who has not laughed while going miniature golfing, singing karaoke, or playing a game where you have to guess what the other team is trying to draw?

You can organize game nights with your friends and family. Perhaps you can dedicate one night of the week for game night. It will give everyone something to look forward to each week. It will be a nice break for everyone to play a game instead of watching yet another cop drama on TV.

Games and fun activities do not have to be just with your friends and family, they could be with your coworkers. If everyone is having a stressful day at work, maybe you can suggest everyone take a break and play a quick game of "Simon Says". Or you can suggest a contest to see who can do the best impression of your boss, when he is out to lunch of course.

Become A Joke Teller

When you find yourself surrounded by stressed out and uptight people, you can be the one to change the mood. You can change the direction of the conversation by simply asking if anyone has heard a good joke lately. Even a dumb joke can lighten the mood in almost any situation, like this one. Two peanuts were walking down the alley and one was assaulted.

If nobody can remember a joke, then you can tell one of yours. When you have some free time, learn a few jokes that are appropriate in all situations. They don't have to be the funniest jokes ever written, but people will appreciate someone trying to liven the mood. Who knows, you might actually be a funny person.

Laughing Calms You Down

It is amazing how an unexpected burst of laughter can defuse a tense situation. When I was a police officer, humor was my special weapon when dealing with angry or upset people. I was shocked at how well it worked. I didn't have them rolling on the floor with my jokes, but my humor was usually enough to deescalate their emotions even temporarily. Then I was able to have a rational discussion with them about what was going on.

Have you ever had a stressful moment and then the tension was relieved by an unexpected moment of laughter? Perhaps you were yelling about the garbage not being taken out and then you look down and notice you are wearing bunny slippers. You can't help but laugh in that moment. You can't be angry while wearing bunny slippers.

In personal relationships, laughter is an underused tool. In times of disagreement, laughter can be the common ground when you feel there is none. If you are fighting with your partner, watch a funny movie together. Show your partner a funny video you saw on social media that day, or get out your laser pointer and take turns making your cat chase it up and down the hallway.

Laughter Is An Aphrodisiac

There is a lot of data that has been gleaned from the numerous online dating sites about the value of humor. They have pinpointed characteristics and traits that people feel are the most important. One of the top characteristics desired is for their partner to be funny.

I am not telling you that you have to be funny or else you will face a life of solitude, but there is a good reason why laughter is so important in forging romantic relationships.

Laughter releases endorphins into your bloodstream. Those endorphins make you feel good. When your partner makes you laugh, they are the cause of you feeling happy. It is no wonder they would want to see you again. They associate feeling good with being in your presence.

Laughing with your partner also allows you to open up and be more comfortable with each other. When things don't seem so serious all the time, people can feel less stressed about potential judgements and criticism. This can lead to a deeper sense of trust, which can lead to more intimacy. So forget the oysters and the red wine, the best aphrodisiac is laughter.

Make Them Laugh And Make The Sale

The same way laughing can help form romantic relationships, it also works in the business world. Instead of your clients falling in love with you though, they will be more receptive to listening to what you or your company can do for them.

It's no wonder why so many great speakers start off with a few jokes. Once the audience starts to laugh, it changes the dynamic of the presentation. It can make the audience relax and not be as judgmental or guarded. When the audience is more comfortable, they will be more receptive to hearing the messages you're going to deliver. Many times it is not what information you are offering, it is how you are delivering it that will be the biggest factor in your success.

Chapter Summary

- Laughter releases endorphins into your body which make you feel good

- Laughter can strengthen your immune system

- Laughter is the universal ice breaker

- Laughter helps build bonds between people

- There are endless ways to add more laughter into your life

- Include laughter into your daily routine

Action Plan

They say that laughter is the best medicine. Make a "Laughter Medicine Cabinet" that is filled with items that make you laugh. They could include your favorite funny movies, joke books, comic books or anything that you find funny. You can also have a virtual laughter medicine cabinet on your smartphone or computer. They could be filled with funny videos and comedy routines from your favorite comedians. Make a list of the items you will put into your laughter medicine cabinet(s).

1. _____

2. _____

3. _____

4. _____

5. _____

6. _____

7. _____

Now whenever you are feeling like you need a little pick me up, you can go to your laughter medicine cabinet and bring a smile back to your face.

Learn a few short jokes that you like and can easily remember. You can find jokes on the internet or in joke books at the library or bookstore. Write down some of your favorite jokes below.

1. _____

_____

_____

_____

2. _____

_____

_____

_____

3. _____

_____

_____

_____

It is always great to have a few jokes ready. You never know when they are going to come in handy. Whether it is to help diffuse a tense situation or just a way to try and brighten someone's day.

Once you are available to laugh at yourself, the world becomes a lighter and brighter place. Appreciate the funny moments in your life. Write down a few funny experiences that you can share with others.

1. _____

   _____

   _____

   _____

2. _____

   _____

   _____

   _____

3. _____

   _____

   _____

   _____

When you are open to showing others that you do not take yourself too seriously, you are allowing others to be more comfortable in your presence. This will allow bonds to quickly form. Laughter is the universal glue that can bring people together.

Daily Action:

1. Look for the laughter in everyday things all around you.

2. Do not take yourself so seriously.

3. Commit to organizing or attending events that lend themselves to laughter.

4. Include laughter in all your relationships.

5. Save things that make you laugh in your laughter medicine cabinet(s).

"Happiness is an inside job."

- William Arthur Ward

Chapter 13: Putting It All Together

Congratulations! You made it all the way through this book. I am proud of you. You are now Living Your Big Juicy Life! That wasn't so hard, was it?

Keep this book handy so that you can go back to it whenever you want. Reading it again can reinforce all that you have learned and you might end up discovering some new "Aha moments".

When you feel like your life is not as sweet as it could be lately, read this overview and see what chapters you can revisit. The principles in this book are timeless and apply for all stages of your life. You can also do the action plans again and see how they have changed since the first time you did them.

Know Where You Are Going

So many of us drift through life and wonder why we end up in places that don't make us happy. Many of us find ourselves shaking our head and saying how did my life end up like this? This isn't where I was supposed to be. It is important to know where you want to go in your life. If you don't know where you are going, that is exactly where you will end up. Nowhere.

Life is fluid and you have the freedom to change your mind, but it is important to at least have a direction. Make sure that on any given day, you are able to answer the question of where are you going in your life. It might seem like a very simple step, but it is vitally important to allow you to always be consciously and subconsciously headed in the right direction.

Do Not Procrastinate

Time is your most valuable asset. Many of us feel like we have unlimited time. The truth is that we do not. Time slips by quite quickly. Don't put things off until tomorrow. Tomorrows are not guaranteed. Take charge of your life by taking action daily. When you are taking action daily, you are in control of your destiny. Remember, just by taking small steps each day, you can achieve big goals.

Since time is so precious, make the most of each day and live in the present moment. The present moment is the only place where we are truly living. It is the only place from where we can take action. It does not serve you to obsess on your past or become fixated on your future. Concentrate on action you can take in the present moment to experience love, joy and success.

Embrace Change

Many of us are automatically resistant to change. Even when we are not happy in our current situations, there is comfort in knowing exactly where we stand. We become fearful it might become worse if we make changes. We don't want to "jump out of the frying pan into the fire". That is not the way to live a Big Juicy Life. Do not be afraid to take risks and make a change that will allow you to have more love, joy and success.

Have fun embracing change. Set an intention to constantly do new things. Do not fall into a pattern of doing the same things over and over again. Add some spice and variety into your life by changing your daily habits and routines. It is through these changes that you will experience pleasant surprises that will give you more opportunities for love, joy and success.

You Can Do Anything

Many times we become doubtful that we can achieve our desires. We become frozen with fear and do not go after our dreams. The truth is you are more capable than you ever imagined. The proof is in your past. There were times when you thought you were not going to be able to do something and yet you succeeded. You overcame your fears and doubts and were successful. Remember this phrase when you doubt yourself. "If you did it once, you can do it again, if you did it again, you can do it all the time."

The way that you can overcome your fears is by believing you can do it. There's no other factor that will be a bigger determinant of whether or not you will be successful. Remember what Henry Ford said, "Whether you think you can or think you can't, you are right." Always have an "I can" attitude. Don't quit and you will be surprised at what you are capable of.

Laugh Every Day

Laughter is the all-natural wonder drug that you can incorporate into your daily life without any negative side effects. Laughing is good for you on all levels. It decreases stress, improves your immune system, and changes your outlook on life to be more positive. There is laughter all around you, you just need to set an intention to see it more often. It is easy to incorporate more laughter into your daily life.

Ask For What You Want

Your ability to ask for what you want is like having the genie from a magic lamp at your disposal. It is truly mind blowing what you can get just by simply asking for it – you have the ability to involve everyone around you in your pursuit of your desires – it is probably the most underused gift that you have in your life.

Be bold in your ability to ask for anything and everything that you want. Remember, the one who asks is the one that gets. When you begin to see the positive results of asking, it is like being a kid in a candy store. Just remember to be grateful and show appreciation to those who help you.

You Are Your Own Guru

We spend so much time looking to others to answer the questions of what we should do in our lives. We have been conditioned to believe that others know what is best for us. The truth is that nobody knows you better than you. You are the best person to know what will be the right choices for you. Learn to quiet your mind and look within for all the answers you seek, you will find them.

Action And Connection Will Bring You Happiness

Many of us get frustrated by not being able to experience happiness in our lives on a consistent basis. We incorrectly believe that we must be more, have more, and get more in order to experience happiness. There is a much better and simpler way to add more happiness to your life.

Action and connection are the two keys that will be able to add more happiness to your life. When you take action, make sure that you are able to feel a positive emotion while you are taking the action. There are endless ways that you can add more action and connection into your life.

Expect A Little, Give A Lot In Relationships

There many different ways that we can judge the value of our relationship. The most important aspect of your relationship is not how much you love the other person or how much they love you; it's how you feel about yourself when you're with that person. You should feel good about yourself in your relationship. You should be able to express yourself fully in all ways, including spiritually, emotionally, sexually and intellectually.

Communication is vital to a good relationship. When dealing with your partner, be honest and upfront with what you are feeling. When you are hurt, be specific in what you are unhappy with. When you are comfortable in speaking from your heart, it means that there is a high level of trust and respect for each other. Good communication can also allow each other's desires to become a reality by feeling comfortable in asking for anything and everything.

The Real Value Of Money

Having a lot of money does not guarantee you will have love, joy and success. It is just a tool for you to use to add more happiness to your life. Money can be spent in many different ways. Often people focus on the accumulation of material goods as the best way to experience happiness. They believe that by accumulating more, they will be happier. That can set you up for a never ending feeling of being unsatisfied and living in a constant state of lack.

Money is best used to have experiences. It is experiences that give you more opportunities for love, joy and success. You can have so many different types of experiences – you can travel, you can go back to school, or you can give to charity – it is up to you to find the ones that resonate with you the most.

You Are Enough

The biggest factor that will determine how much love, joy and success you will experience in your life is the way you feel about yourself. If you feel like you are not enough, you will be forever seeking someone or something that will convince you that you are good enough. You must realize that the only person who can make you feel like you are enough is you.

The truth is you are lovable, wonderful and are definitely good enough. You are worthy of all you desire. You can change your negative beliefs by challenging them and see how they do not stand up to scrutiny. When you begin to adopt new, more positive beliefs, soon you will have a sense of self-worth that nobody can take away from you or diminish. It is only then that you will be capable of reaching your true potential and be able to live the life of your dreams.

Action Plan

Write down the 5 biggest "Aha moments" you experienced while reading this book.

1. _____

2. _____

3. _____

4. _____

5. _____

Do not forget these "Aha moments" as you go through your daily life. Make sure you are incorporating this new knowledge into your Big Juicy Life. Sometimes we feel like we have unlocked something that will help us, but we do not hold onto it and reinforce its use. It seems like we quickly forget about it and revert back to our old ways. Don't do that! Embrace your new knowledge and use it to keep moving forward!

List the 5 best moments you experienced from following the action plans in this book.

1. _____

2. _____

3. _____

4. _____

5. _____

It is amazing how making even small changes in our lives can have such a huge impact. Do not underestimate the power of taking different action in your life. If you have not done some of the action plans in this book, revisit them and see if you feel more comfortable in trying them now.

Daily Action:

LIVE YOUR BIG JUICY LIFE!

Epilogue

Thank you for purchasing this book. I hope you enjoyed it and it made your life a little better than before you picked it up. If you would like to go deeper with Living Your Big Juicy Life, I offer individual Life Coaching which can help you live the life of your dreams. I am also a Certified Infinite Possibilities Trainer™ and can facilitate this life changing program either in person or online. It is great for groups as well as individuals. For more information, feel free to email me at Michael@LivingYourBigJuicyLife.com. I look forward to hearing from you.

Also check out my website to purchase "I Love My Big Juicy Life" wristbands and other gear to celebrate living the life of your dreams! **LivingYourBigJuicyLife.com**

About The Author

Michael Tarby is a true Renaissance Man. He has made more mistakes than most, but has learned much from his life experiences. He has been everything from a police officer to an actor. He has held every job imaginable, except for rodeo clown, but he does have an application pending.

He has been an overachiever most of his life, graduating from college with a 4.0 GPA, being the class president and winning several awards and scholarships.

Michael has always been a caring person. In the third grade, he won the Junior Psychiatrists Award for helping fellow students suffering from multiplication anxiety. More recently, he cofounded a charity which raised over $33,000 to help a friend pay for her cancer treatment.

Michael is an author, speaker, and life coach. He has created and presented several of his own programs including

"How to Be Authentic", "What Are Your Wishes?" and "Tired of Bad Relationships, Let's Explore You".

He recently received a standing ovation from an international audience of over 240 people. He has helped hundreds of people live happier and more fulfilled lives. Contact him today to see how he can help you live the life of your dreams.

Email: Michael@LivingYourBigJuicyLife.com

Made in the USA
Columbia, SC
30 October 2020

23766579R00146